TECHNICAL REPORT

The Dynamic Retention Model for Air Force Officers

New Estimates and Policy Simulations of the Aviator Continuation Pay Program

Michael Mattock, Jeremy Arkes

Prepared for the United States Air Force

RAND PROJECT AIR FORCE

The research described in this report was sponsored by the United States Air Force under Contracts FA7014-06-C-0001 and F49642-01-C-0003. Further information may be obtained from the Strategic Planning Division, Directorate of Plans, Hq USAF.

Library of Congress Cataloging-in-Publication Data

Mattock, Michael G., 1961-
The dynamic retention model for Air Force officers : new estimates and policy simulations of the aviator continuation pay program / Michael Mattock, Jeremy Arkes.
p. cm.
Includes bibliographical references.
ISBN 978-0-8330-4158-6 (pbk. : alk. paper)
1. United States. Air Force—Recruiting, enlistment, etc. 2. United States. Air Force—Pay, allowances, etc.
I. Arkes, Jeremy. II. Title.

UG883.M38 2007
358.4'332—dc22

2007027895

The RAND Corporation is a nonprofit research organization providing objective analysis and effective solutions that address the challenges facing the public and private sectors around the world. RAND's publications do not necessarily reflect the opinions of its research clients and sponsors.

RAND® is a registered trademark.

Published 2007 by the RAND Corporation
1776 Main Street, P.O. Box 2138, Santa Monica, CA 90407-2138
1200 South Hayes Street, Arlington, VA 22202-5050
4570 Fifth Avenue, Suite 600, Pittsburgh, PA 15213-2665
RAND URL: http://www.rand.org/
To order RAND documents or to obtain additional information, contact
Distribution Services: Telephone: (310) 451-7002;
Fax: (310) 451-6915; Email: order@rand.org

Preface

The U.S. Air Force (USAF) needs to attract, promote, and retain the appropriate quantity and quality (e.g., experience level) of officers to execute current and future missions. The pay and promotion system is a key tool in officer retention efforts. The USAF needs to be able to assess the probable effects of changes in pay and promotion policies on the future retention of USAF officers before actually implementing proposed changes.

Therefore, the Air Force is interested in models that can simulate the effects changes in pay and promotion policy might have on officer retention. This technical report documents a particular type of model, the dynamic retention model (DRM) developed by Glenn A. Gotz and John Joseph McCall in *A Dynamic Retention Model for Air Force Officers: Theory and Estimates*, RAND Corporation, R-3028-AF, 1984, and the extension of the basic DRM to take into account the effect of the availability of multiyear contracts to certain classes of Air Force officers. Unlike other models, the DRM takes into account the value an officer may place on future career flexibility and thus is particularly well suited to examining the effect of bonus programs that have service commitments, such as the Aviator Continuation Pay (ACP) program.

The model described in this report was initially developed for a fiscal year (FY) 2003 project, "Officer Retention and Experience," sponsored by Lt Gen Roger A. Brady, Deputy Chief of Staff, Personnel, Headquarters U.S. Air Force (AF/A1). The research was conducted in the Manpower, Personnel, and Training Program of RAND Project AIR FORCE. The report should interest those involved in Air Force officer personnel management and those with an interest in modeling to support development of personnel policies.

RAND Project AIR FORCE

RAND Project AIR FORCE (PAF), a division of the RAND Corporation, is the U.S. Air Force's federally funded research and development center for studies and analyses. PAF provides the Air Force with independent analyses of policy alternatives affecting the development, employment, combat readiness, and support of current and future aerospace forces. Research is conducted in four programs: Aerospace Force Development; Manpower, Personnel, and Training; Resource Management; and Strategy and Doctrine.

Additional information about PAF is available on our Web site at
http://www.rand.org/paf/

Contents

Preface ... iii
Figures ... vii
Tables ... ix
Summary ... xi
Acknowledgments ... xiii
Abbreviations ... xv

CHAPTER ONE
Introduction ... 1
Background ... 1
Objective and Research Approach ... 2
How This Report Is Organized ... 2

CHAPTER TWO
A Dynamic Retention Model ... 3
Modeling the Value of Flexibility—An Example ... 5
Relation of the Dynamic Retention Model to the Aviator Continuation Pay Program ... 5
A Retention Model ... 6
Modeling Uncertainty—Taste ... 7
Modeling Uncertainty—Shocks ... 8
Concluding Remarks ... 10

CHAPTER THREE
Comparing the Dynamic Retention Model and the Annualized Cost of Leaving Family of Models ... 11
A Simplified DRM ... 11
Modeling a Five-Year Commitment ... 12
The Annualized Cost of Leaving 2 Model ... 13

CHAPTER FOUR
Results of the Dynamic Retention Model ... 17
Estimating the Parameters ... 17
Model Estimates ... 17

Simulations Based on the Estimates 18
Comparison with the Estimates of Gotz and McCall 21
Conclusions 22

APPENDIXES
A. Implementation Details and Model Estimates 23
B. Computer Program and Data 45

Bibliography 67

Figures

2.1. Influences on Individual Retention Decisions 4
2.2. Simple Retention Model 6
2.3. Modeling Uncertainty 7
2.4. Distribution of Taste for Military Service in Pilot ROTC Graduates 9
2.5. Change in Taste for Service 9
2.6. Distribution of Environmental Shock for Pilots 10
4.1. Observed and Predicted Pilot Retention Rates 18
4.2. Observed and Predicted Pilot Retention Rates for Non-ROTC Accessions 19
4.3. Observed and Predicted Pilot Retention Rates for ROTC Accessions 19
4.4. Simulating the Effect of a 10-Percent Pay Cut for Pilots 20
4.5. Simulated Effect of Eliminating the 20-Year Option for Pilots 21
4.6. Simulating Elimination of the ACP Program for Pilots 21
A.1. R Implementation of the ACP DRM 34
A.2. Observed and Predicted Retention Rates for Mission Support Officers 38
A.3. DRM and ACOL 2 Predicted Cumulative Retention Rates for Pilots 39
A.4. DRM and ACOL 2 Predicted-Actual Cumulative Continuation Rates for Pilots 39
A.5. DRM and ACOL Simulations of the Effect of a 10-Percent Pay Cut for Pilots 40
A.6. DRM and ACOL Simulations of the Effect of Eliminating the 20-Year Option for Pilots 41
A.7. DRM and ACOL Simulations of the Effect of Eliminating ACP for Pilots 41
A.8. DRM and ACOL 2 Predicted Cumulative Retention Rates for Mission Support Officers 42
A.9. DRM and ACOL Simulations of the Effect of 10-Percent Pay Cut for Mission Support Officers 42

Tables

A.1. MLE Estimates for Pilot ACP DRM 36
A.2. MLE Estimates for Mission Support Officers 37
B.1. Data Dictionary for Pilot Data 62
B.2. Pilot Data 62

Summary

All the military services face problems retaining the number of quality officers they need to support current and future needs. In the USAF, the problem is most acute in the case of pilots, information technology specialists, scientists, and engineers. The USAF developed a pay incentive program to induce pilots to remain in the service. The ACP program pays an annual bonus to pilots who commit to certain terms of service. The ACP program has been expanded to certain groups of navigators and air battle managers. Generally the bonuses are paid to officers who agree to extend their service for specified numbers of years (e.g., three or five) or to a specified length of service, (e.g., 25 years of aviation service [YAS]).

Accurate models are needed to help the USAF develop retention policies that will retain a sufficient number of officers having the right qualities. The Air Force, and researchers working on personnel issues for the Air Force and other services, have long used an annualized cost of leaving (ACOL) model to help determine how changes in compensation would affect retention. However, the ACOL model does not handle two important factors in retention decisions particularly well: future uncertainty and random "shocks."

The advantage of the DRM is that it allows us to model how officers might value future career flexibility in the face of uncertainty. This is important in evaluating how people will respond to contracts that obligate them to multiple years of service, such as those available under the ACP program. Advances in computer hardware and software have now made estimation of the DRM feasible on even low-end personal computers.

The DRM can be used to explore different policy options by taking individual retention decisions and running them through various policy alternatives. For example, it can analyze the effect of proposed changes to the ACP program, such as eliminating the until-20-YAS option or the elimination of the ACP program altogether. The DRM shows that eliminating the until-20-YAS option (while keeping the five-year contract option) results in only a small change to overall retention, while eliminating the ACP program altogether would result in the Air Force losing up to 15 percent of its most experienced officers.[1]

We have included the full model code and associated data in Appendix B; this should enable workers in the field of officer retention to readily replicate the results reported here,

[1] As of FY 2005, the until-20-YAS option is no longer available, and only initially eligible officers can take the five-year option.

enhance and extend the model, and run simulations exploring different policy alternatives (e.g., changes to the retirement system) from those covered in this technical report.

Conclusions

The DRM fits the data. Our extension of the DRM to cover ACP offers the Air Force an effective tool with which to analyze how officers respond to multiyear agreements. Computer code is now readily available to implement the model. We recommend that the Air Force adopt the model and consider widening its application.

Acknowledgments

The authors would like to acknowledge the help of Glenn Gotz, Craig Moore, and especially Maj Kevin Therrien, Chief of Rated-Force Policy for Mobile Forces, U.S. Air Force, all of whom provided timely advice, feedback, and salient examples for demonstrating the capabilities of the DRM. We would also like to thank Al Robbert, Jim Hosek, John Ausink, Beth Asch, and Jerry Sollinger, who provided advice and encouragement during the long gestation of this technical report.

This report is dedicated to the memory of Glenn Gotz, who passed away during its preparation. We hope that this report will lead to a wider recognition and appreciation of the fundamental contribution that his work in collaboration with John McCall made to econometrics in general and military manpower research in particular. He was a man truly ahead of his time. He will be sorely missed.

Abbreviations

ABM	air battle manager
ACOL	annualized cost of leaving
ACP	aviator continuation pay
BFGS	Broyden-Fletcher-Goldfarb-Shanno
CPS	Current Population Survey
DRM	dynamic retention model
EM	expectation-maximization
FY	fiscal year
GEM	generalized expectation-maximization
MAP	maximum a priori
MLE	maximum likelihood estimator
PAF	Project AIR FORCE
ROTC	Reserve Officer Training Corps
USAF	United States Air Force
YAS	years of aviation service
YOS	years of service

CHAPTER ONE

Introduction

Background

In testimony before the House Armed Services Committee in July 2001, the Chief of Staff of the Air Force cited retention as the most pressing problem facing the Air Force. Retaining pilots, information technology specialists, scientists, and engineers was proving particularly difficult. Several years ago, the Air Force developed a pay incentive program to induce pilots to remain in the service: The Aviator Continuation Pay (ACP) program paid an annual bonus to pilots who committed to certain terms of service.[1] Subsequently, the program was expanded to include not only pilots but also certain groups of navigators and air battle managers (ABMs). ACP agreements are now offered to navigators with at least 15 years of aviation service (YAS) and 18 or more years of total active-duty military service. Eligible navigators are offered three-year agreements at $10,000 per year, five-year agreements at $15,000 per year, and agreements that they complete 25 years of aviation service at $15,000 per year. Navigators with 20 or more years of aviation service are eligible to commit to three years of service at the low rate, $10,000 per year, or to agree to remain until they have completed 25 years of aviation service at the high rate, $15,000 per year, if the agreement is greater than three years.

The Air Force and researchers working for the Air Force have long used an annualized cost of leaving (ACOL) model to help to determine how officers would react to pay raises, and it worked relatively well for that purpose. However, analyzing the effects of incentives such as the ACP program is a more complicated endeavor: It is not simply a matter of modeling reactions to a pay raise but also must account for the effects of forgoing other options. In the case of a pilot, for example, remaining in the Air Force under an ACP agreement means that he or she is giving up the opportunity to fly civilian airliners. The ACOL family of models does not allow modeling the value that pilots would place on future career flexibility, hence a new model is needed.

[1] Department of the Air Force, *Aviator Continuation Pay (ACP) Program*, Air Force Instruction 36-3004, Washington, D.C., February 24, 2000.

Objective and Research Approach

To develop a set of retention policies that would retain the right number and quality of officers wanted, researchers need to model how people make retention decisions in an uncertain world. This research project took an approach based on the Gotz-McCall dynamic retention model (DRM),[2] extending the basic DRM to cover the possibility of Air Force officers entering into multiyear contracts in exchange for greater pay.

How This Report Is Organized

Chapter Two describes the characteristics and logic of the DRM. Chapter Three compares the DRM with the ACOL model, and Chapter Four presents the modeling results. Appendix A gives the estimates produced by the model, and Appendix B presents the computer code and data used to estimate the model.

---

[2] Glenn A. Gotz and John Joseph McCall, *A Dynamic Retention Model for Air Force Officers: Theory and Estimates*, Santa Monica, Calif.: RAND Corporation, R-3028-AF, 1984.

CHAPTER TWO

A Dynamic Retention Model

The dynamic retention modeling technique has been available since the late 1970s, but it has been difficult to use because it is computationally intensive. Advances in both computing software and hardware over the last two decades have eliminated this drawback. Using the DRM, we developed a method for statistically estimating model parameters using historical officer data and simulating the effect of changes in personnel policies on retention.

A key attribute of this approach is that it focuses on individual behavior. Figure 2.1 shows our concept of the decision process leading to a decision to stay or leave. Two aspects of the figure merit comment. One is that individual retention decisions result from a complex interaction of many influences. Certainly, Air Force compensation policies influence a service person's decision to stay or leave. However, the strength of that influence varies depending on the individual. An officer who really enjoys military service (has a "taste" for it) might elect to remain in the service for less compensation than would an individual with less of a taste for service. External influences are important as well. If the civilian job market is robust and the individual's skills are in demand, then the motivation to leave would be relatively greater than if the market is poor or the individual's skills are not prized. A second point worthy of comment (which might seem obvious) is that aggregate or group behavior is driven by individual decisions. Looking at how individuals make decisions gives us more insight into the retention process than does studying only the mythical "average" officer.

It is important to focus on the behavior of specific individuals in order to arrive at parameter estimates that describe the preferences of officers with regard to key aspects of their environment. This is opposed to the typical models, which describe an average response to an external influence; this average response is the end result of a traditional regression model. Using the DRM, we model an officer's decision process and take into account individuals' attempts to optimize their futures. By modeling individual decisions, any given parameter estimate is less dependent on specific policies in effect during the period covered by the data than it would be using the ACOL method. For example, the DRM examines the effect of both direct pay and pay that is contingent upon a commitment to stay in the Air Force for a given time period. Although an individual might find a salary increase of $10,000 per year quite attractive, if accompanied by an obligation to continue to serve for five more years, it might not be enough to induce him or her to remain in the service. If we construct a model of the internal decision-making process of an Air Force pilot that takes into account regular military pay, ACP, and civilian career opportunities, then estimates of the remaining parameters depend less on these

Figure 2.1
Influences on Individual Retention Decisions

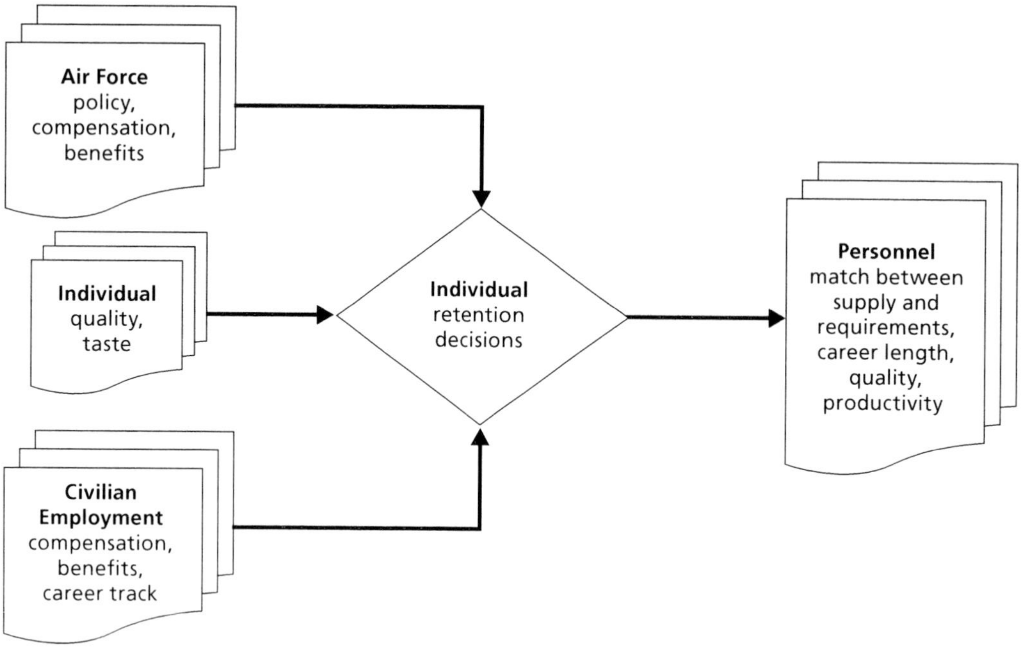

RAND TR470 2.1

factors. This type of model can be used to predict the effect of a broader range of compensation and personnel policy options. On the other hand, if we construct a retention model for Air Force pilots that did not include the ACP program in the officer's decisionmaking calculus, then the estimates provided by that model could be used with confidence only if all aspects of the ACP remained unchanged, because the estimated parameters implicitly depend on the specifics of the ACP program in effect during the period covered by the data used to estimate the parameters of the model. (By specifics we mean, for example, the amount of the annual bonus, the amount of the lump sum payment that can be given to officers up-front under some agreements, and the length of the obligated term of service.) Many traditional regression models fall into this category.

Explicitly modeling individual behavior also allows for the fact that individuals are different. People's behavior can differ as a result of both observable and unobservable characteristics. For example, an officer's decision to stay in the military can be affected both by his or her particular promotion history (an observable characteristic) or his or her taste for military service (an unobservable characteristic). The DRM allows for differences in both observed and unobserved characteristics, whereas traditional regression models typically allow for differences only in observable characteristics.

One of the key features of the DRM is that it explicitly models an officer's decision calculus as taking into account future uncertainty. (Other models of retention, such as ACOL, ACOL 2, or the Ausink and Wise "option value" model, do not explicitly include future uncertainty in the officer's decision calculus.) Including uncertainty enables us to model flexibility—

the ability to make or change decisions when new information comes to light. This is sometimes referred to as an option value and is a common concept to those who trade in securities. The ability to buy or sell an option at a particular price has value: It enables a person to hedge risk. A concrete example may help illustrate this point.

Modeling the Value of Flexibility—An Example

Consider the case of betting on a coin flip. A "heads" means that the individual wins \$1, and a "tails" means \$0. Thus, the expected value of the bet is

$$\frac{1}{2}\$1.00 + \frac{1}{2}\$0.00 = \$0.50$$

Now consider a case in which (1) there are two coins that each have an equal chance of coming up heads or tails and (2) the bettor can chose either coin *before* it is flipped. The expected value from choosing a coin is the same as that in the example above, \$0.50. However, now consider the case where the bettor can choose between the two coins *after* they are flipped. If both come up heads, the bettor can choose either one and receive \$1. If only one comes up heads, the bettor can choose that one and still receive \$1. If both come up tails, then the bettor receives nothing. The expected value of this bet is \$0.75 because three times out of four the bettor can receive \$1. The following formula describes this result:

$$\frac{1}{4}\$1.00 + \frac{1}{4}\$1.00 + \frac{1}{4}\$1.00 + \frac{1}{4}\$0.00 = \$0.75$$

So the ability to make an informed choice has an expected value of \$0.25 (\$0.75 – \$0.50 = \$0.25). If all anyone cared about was the expected value of the return on the bet, then in order to get him or her to give up the opportunity to choose after the coins had been flipped, they would have to be compensated by at least \$0.25 because the value of the bet with no choice (\$0.50) plus compensation for losing the opportunity to choose (\$0.25) would just equal the value of a bet with choice (\$0.75).[1]

Relation of the Dynamic Retention Model to the Aviator Continuation Pay Program

Similarly, if we want to contract officers to stay for an additional five years, we would need to compensate them for the value of the future choices they are giving up. A five-year contract means that they would have to forgo any opportunities that they could take advantage of only

[1] The authors would like to thank James R. Hosek for this example.

by leaving the military during that period of time. This compensation may have to be quite sizable to make people indifferent to the opportunities that they may be forgoing by entering into a five-year contract, particularly if they can continue to serve on a year-to-year basis. To get a retention effect for the marginal officer (that is, an officer who is indifferent between staying and leaving, all other things being equal), we would need to compensate in excess of the option value.

The exact value of the option value will depend on the size of the random shocks (variation in civilian opportunities, health events, etc.) officers are subject to year to year. Officers can experience random shocks from both the civilian and the military side. On the military side, an officer may receive a good or bad assignment, may be passed over for promotion, and so on. On the civilian side, an officer may have the opportunity to take a high-paying civilian position, may see that civilian job opportunities have declined, may find that he or she needs to leave the service to care for an ailing parent, and so on. While we cannot directly observe the distribution of these shocks, we can statistically infer distribution of the difference between the military and civilian shocks in terms of dollars by using the DRM. In general this distribution will differ for pilots, navigators, and ABMs due to the differences in civilian opportunities for officers in these three career fields.

A Retention Model

Figure 2.2 depicts a simple retention model.[2] In this model, each officer makes a decision at the beginning of the period to either stay or leave. If the officer stays, he or she collects the benefits associated with remaining in the military for a year, including the value of the option to stay or leave at the next decision point. If the officer leaves, he or she gets the value of a civilian career path starting in that period. In this simple model behavior is deterministic. This model implicitly assumes that officers with identical observable characteristics would behave identically. It takes no account of the possibility that nominally identical officers might make different decisions about whether to stay or leave.

Figure 2.2
Simple Retention Model

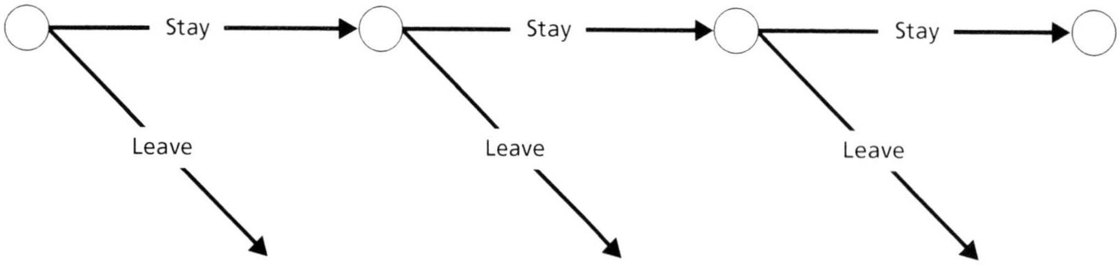

RAND *TR470-2.2*

[2] This discussion parallels the discussion in Gotz and McCall, 1984.

Modeling Uncertainty—Taste

This simple retention model is a start, but it is insufficient for our purposes as it does not allow for differences among individuals. Allowing for differences in individual retention behavior requires the modeling of uncertainty. Figure 2.3 depicts a more sophisticated model that injects uncertainty and takes into account differences in individuals' characteristics or in the environment that an individual faces.

Figure 2.3
Modeling Uncertainty

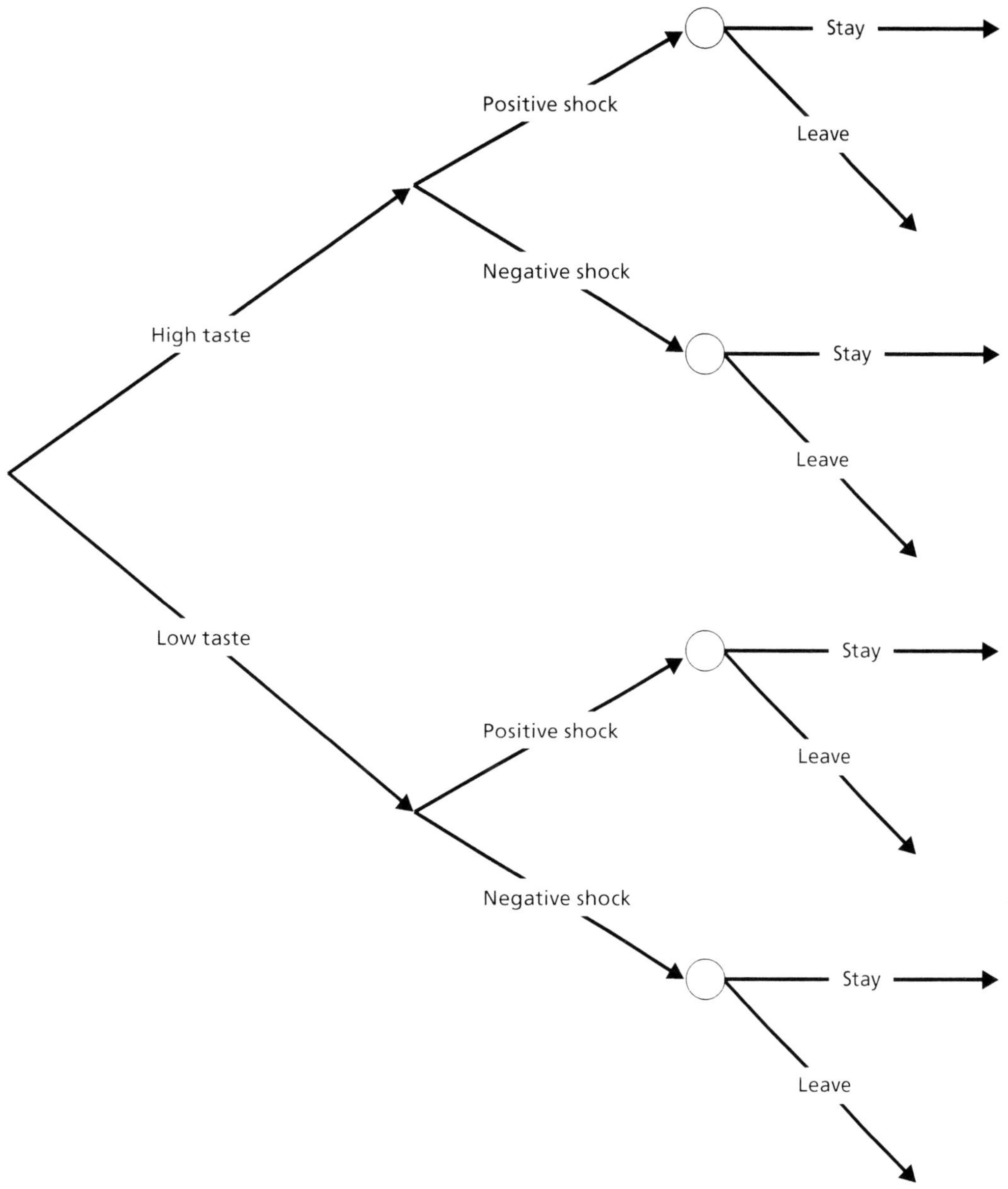

RAND *TR470-2.3*

In this example, both the individual being modeled and the analyst face uncertainty. It begins with an individual who has a certain taste for military service. ("Taste" in this case is used to describe how much or how little someone likes a job or a career.) We assume that an individual is aware of his or her taste for military service, and makes decisions accordingly, but that this taste is not known to the analyst. The individual then experiences a positive or a negative shock. The value of the shock is unknown in advance to either the officer or the analyst. The shock affects the value the individual places on staying in the military until the next decision. The shock can make an individual place either a higher value on staying (a positive shock) or a lower value on staying (a negative shock). Thus the analyst faces uncertainty over both the value that a particular individual places on staying in the military and on the value of the shock he or she might experience in any given period.

One analytical approach to this problem is to assume that taste is distributed across a population according to some parameterized distribution and then to estimate the parameters of the taste distribution in a statistical model. Figure 2.4 presents one such estimate, in this case developed for pilots who graduated from the Reserve Officer Training Corps (ROTC).

The figure shows the estimated distribution of the taste for military service held by the population of ROTC accession pilots when they reach their first stay/leave decision point. The dollar values shown represent the monetary equivalent of the intrinsic value an individual places on a year of military service (in addition to compensation and other benefits). An officer with a strong taste for military service would require relatively more money to be induced to leave than an officer with a weak taste. This curve reflects the initial distribution of taste for the group. The shape of this curve will change over time as officers leave the service. That change is reflected in the curves displayed in Figure 2.5, which shows how the population distribution of taste changes over time.

Figure 2.5 shows that the population distribution of taste for service increases with tenure for a notional officer population. This is relatively intuitive, since those who value service in the Air Force will tend to stay longer. The chart shows less taste for service among those with 6 years of service (the curve farthest to the left), the greatest taste among those with 19 years of service (the curve farthest to the right), and taste distributions gradually shifting from left to right with each successive year of service.

Modeling Uncertainty—Shocks

Figure 2.6 shows that officers will experience different types of shocks (which, as we noted earlier, are unanticipated events that will affect their desire to remain in the Air Force). These shocks can be positive or negative. A positive shock is one that strengthens their preference for the Air Force and a negative shock is one that has the opposite effect. Officers who choose to leave the Air Force forgo the possibility of future positive shocks (e.g., a desirable assignment, an accelerated promotion, the opportunity to train on a new model of aircraft). The model assumes that the shocks are independently and identically distributed across the population.

Figure 2.4
Distribution of Taste for Military Service in Pilot ROTC Graduates

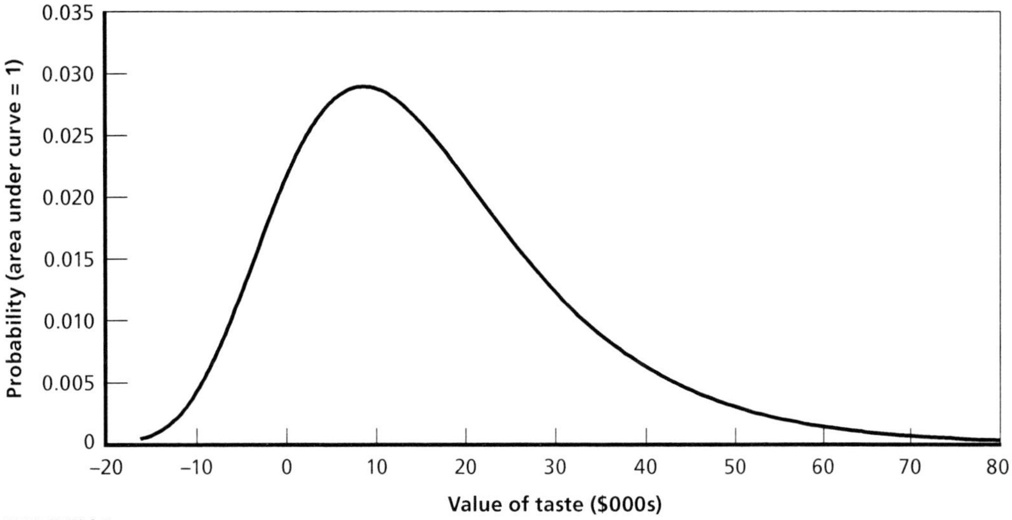

RAND *TR470-2.4*

Figure 2.5
Change in Taste for Service

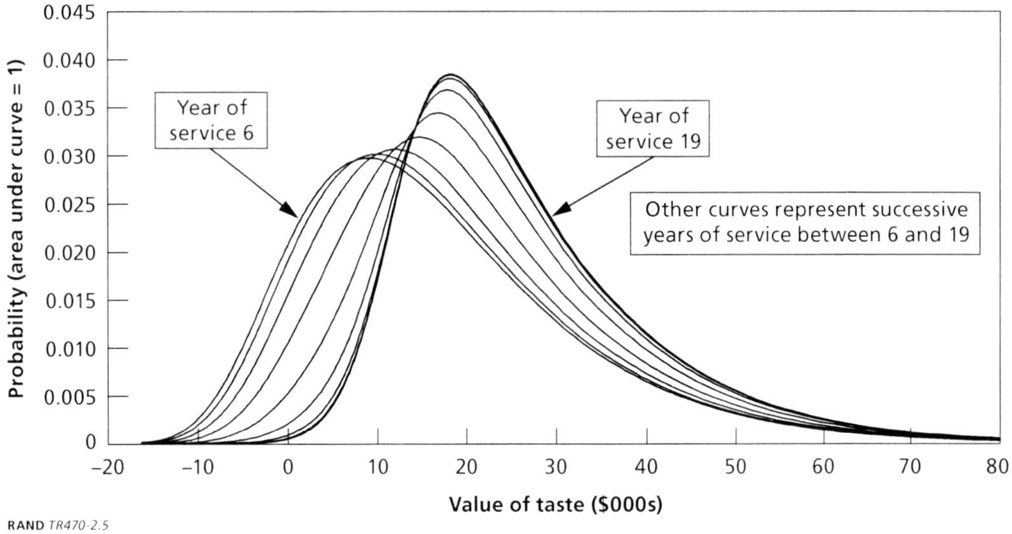

RAND *TR470-2.5*

Figure 2.6
Distribution of Environmental Shock for Pilots

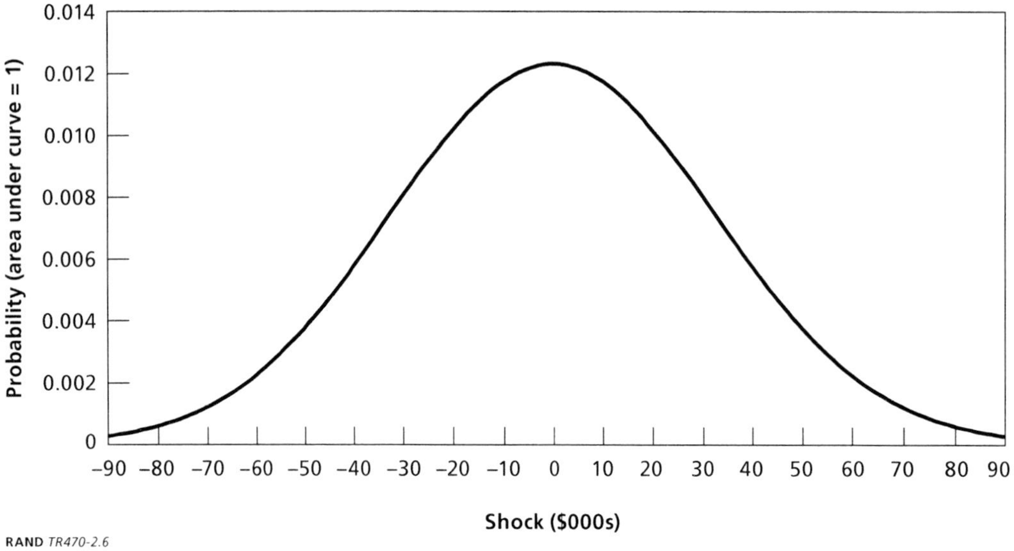

RAND *TR470-2.6*

Concluding Remarks

Modeling individual behavior requires modeling uncertainty explicitly. The individual components of uncertainty include elements that are known to the officer but unknown to the analyst, such as individual taste. The components of uncertainty also include elements that are unknown to both the officer and the analyst, such as future environmental shocks and future promotions. By modeling how these elements affect an individual officer's decisionmaking process we can gain a better understanding of how an officer might value future career flexibility in the face of uncertainty.

CHAPTER THREE

Comparing the Dynamic Retention Model and the Annualized Cost of Leaving Family of Models

Currently, the DRM is not widely used to analyze manpower policy questions, in part because of the computational complexity of the model. The ACOL model devised by John Warner and others provides many of the benefits of the DRM with considerably less computational burden. So, before proceeding further in discussing the specific implementation of the DRM in the case at hand, it might be useful to give some context by comparing it to the ACOL model.

Before comparing the DRM to the ACOL model, it is useful to first describe a simplified version of the DRM, which can then be compared to a corresponding ACOL model. The DRM presented below is simplified by assuming that promotion is deterministic—that is, that individuals are promoted in a given year to the next rank with certainty—and by leaving out covariates such as educational attainment, race, and gender. We present two versions of the model. In the first, the officer can choose only between staying and leaving. The second, more complex model expands the choice set to allow an officer to contract for an additional five years (similar to the plan offered to ABMs in 2004).

A Simplified DRM

The equation used to model the value of leaving is that given in Equation 3.1:

$$V_t^L = W_t^c + \sum_{\tau=t+1}^{T} \beta^{\tau-t} W_\tau^c + R_t^m + \varepsilon_t^c \tag{3.1}$$

Where

V_t^L is the value of leaving at time t,

W_t^c is civilian earnings at time t,

$\sum_{\tau=t+1}^{T} \beta^{\tau-t} W_\tau^c$ is the value of future civilian earnings (where β is the annual discount rate),

R_t^m is the retirement benefit accruing to the officer if he or she leaves at time t, and

ε_t^c is random civilian shock at time t.

The value of leaving depends on current and expected future civilian earnings, retirement benefits, and random shocks. Retirement benefits depend on when retirement occurs.

The value of staying is modeled in Equation 3.2:

$$V_t^S = \gamma^m + W_t^m + \beta \; \mathrm{E}_t[\mathrm{Max}(V_{t+1}^L, V_{t+1}^S)] + \varepsilon_t^m \tag{3.2}$$

Where

V_t^S is the value of staying at time t,

γ^m is individual taste for the Air Force,

W_t^m is military earnings in the current period t, including retirement benefits that will accrue to the officer for staying until t,

$\beta \; \mathrm{E}_t[\mathrm{Max}(V_{t+1}^L, V_{t+1}^S)]$ is the discounted expected value of having the option to choose to stay or leave in the future, with β being the discount rate, and

ε_t^m is the random military shock at time t.

The individual will decide to stay in the military if the value of staying is greater than the value of leaving. If a probability distribution is set for the difference between the random military shock and the random civilian shock, the probability that an individual officer with a particular taste will stay can be computed. Suitably aggregating[1] across all officers in the group of interest will yield predicted retention rates by year of service. These rates can then be tested against historical data on officer stay or leave decisions. Using statistical techniques such as maximum likelihood or simulated method of moments, the parameters for the taste and shock distributions can be estimated.

Modeling a Five-Year Commitment

The model can be expanded to allow the officer the choice to commit for an additional five years. This takes two "stay" equations: one for a one-year commitment that enables an officer to choose from options available at the end of one year and one that allows the officer to choose only from options available at the end of five years.

The first formula appears in Equation 3.3:

$$V_t^{S1} = \gamma^m + W_t^m + \beta \; \mathrm{E}_t[\mathrm{Max}(V_{t+1}^L, V_{t+1}^{S1}, V_{t+1}^{S5})] + \varepsilon_t^m \tag{3.3}$$

Where

V_t^{S1} is the value of staying,

γ^m is individual taste for the Air Force,

[1] That is, integrating out individual taste heterogeneity.

W_t^m is military earnings in the current year, including retirement benefits that will accrue to the officer for staying until t, and

$\beta\ E_t[\mathrm{Max}(V_{t+1}^L, V_{t+1}^{S1}, V_{t+1}^{S5})]$ is the discounted expected value of having the option to choose to stay for one year, to stay for five years, or to leave one year in the future, where

β is the annual discount rate, and

ε_t^m is the random military shock.

The value of contracting for five years is captured in Equation 3.4:

$$V_t^{S5} = \sum_{\tau=t}^{t+4} \beta^{\tau-t}(\gamma^m + W_\tau^{m5}) + \beta^5 E_t[\mathrm{Max}(V_{t+5}^L, V_{t+5}^{S1}, V_{t+5}^{S5})] + \varepsilon_t^m \tag{3.4}$$

Where

V_t^{S5} is the value of the five-year contract,

$\sum_{\tau=t}^{t+4} \beta^{\tau-t}(\gamma^m + W_\tau^{m5})$ is the discounted present value of military earnings including the bonus for the five-year contract (the W_τ^{m5} term),

$\beta^5 E_t[\mathrm{Max}(V_{t+5}^L, V_{t+5}^{S1}, V_{t+5}^{S5})]$ is the discounted present value of the expected value of having the option to choose to stay for one year, to stay for five years, or to leave at a point five years in the future, and

ε_t^m is the random military shock.

If an officer makes the decision to stay, he or she is locked in for one or five years, at which time another decision must be made.

This model can also be expanded in a similar fashion to allow for the choice of a program that requires a service commitment to 20 or 25 years.

The Annualized Cost of Leaving 2 Model

We turn next to the ACOL 2 model and compare it with the DRM. But first some historical background.

The ACOL model was originally developed by John Warner in response to the creation of the DRM by Glenn Gotz and John McCall. At the time the DRM was originally created it was pushing the limits of the capabilities of even the fastest computers. The model was so computationally intensive that in their original paper, Gotz and McCall only presented estimates from a partial maximum likelihood estimator and did not present standard errors. The ACOL model uses an ingenious approximation to compute the relative value of a military career as compared to a civilian career. The approximation was to compute the maximum of the expected value of a military career versus a civilian career, rather than the expected value of the maximum. (This means that the officer is assumed to be unable to make an informed decision when new information is revealed. For example, in our earlier coin flip example, this would correspond to using the maximum of the expected value of the two coin flips—\$0.50—rather than the expected value of the maximum—\$0.75.) This approximation resulted in a model that the computer hardware and software available at the time could easily run. The ACOL model generally provides a good fit for existing data on officer and enlisted personnel retention and has since been widely used. (John Ausink and David Wise also proposed a model that uses a different formulation but essentially the same approximation, i.e., exchanging the expectation and the maximization operators; this model has not seen as much use as ACOL because of its computational complexity.[2]) The basic ACOL model has since been enhanced to include individual heterogeneity in taste (ACOL 2), but the enhanced model still uses the same approximation.

The approximation means that ACOL models officers as if they place no value on future career flexibility. Under ACOL, the decisionmaker acts as if the future is known with certainty; if the future is known with certainty, then the officer knows exactly when he or she will want to leave the Air Force. If there is no uncertainty, then there is no value in keeping options open, such as the option to leave the service at will. Thus, for example, under ACOL, officers are modeled as if they would be willing to take multiyear contracts without any associated bonus, as long as the multiyear contract ends before they plan to leave the service. The ACOL model implies that the officers would not demand any extra compensation in exchange for giving up future options.

Here is a slightly more formal treatment of ACOL. In this discussion, the ACOL 2 model is simplified in that the covariates are not included. The equation for the value of leaving in the ACOL 2 model is

$$V_t^L = W_t^c + \sum_{\tau=t+1}^{T} \beta^{\tau-t} W_\tau^c + R_t^m + \varepsilon_t^c \tag{3.5}$$

This is identical to the equation for the DRM.

The equation for the value of staying in the ACOL 2 model is

$$V_t^S = \gamma^m + W_t^m + \beta \ \mathrm{Max}[\mathrm{E}_t(V_{t+1}^L), \mathrm{E}_t(V_{t+1}^S)] + \varepsilon_t^m \tag{3.6}$$

Where

$\beta \ \mathrm{Max}[\mathrm{E}_t(V_{t+1}^L), \mathrm{E}_t(V_{t+1}^S)]$ is the discounted maximum of the expected value of staying or leaving.

[2] John A. Ausink and David A. Wise, "The Military Pension, Compensation, and Retirement of U.S. Air Force Pilots," Cambridge, Mass.: National Bureau of Economic Research, Working Paper No. W4593, December 1993.

The key difference from the DRM is that the ACOL is computing the maximum of the expected values rather than the expected value of the maximum. This model approximates $E_t[\text{Max}(V_{t+1}^L, V_{t+1}^S)]$ by $\text{Max}(E_t[V_{t+1}^L], E_t[V_{t+1}^S])$. It exchanges the expectation and maximization operators. This is the feature that makes the ACOL models so tractable in comparison to the DRM. The distributions of ε_t^m and ε_t^c are assumed to have mean zero, so the stochastic terms simply drop out of the expressions for the value of staying and the value of leaving for all future periods. This means that computation is much easier, because the model now assumes that the future is certain.

Of course this simplification comes with a cost. This model of decisionmaking does not take into account uncertainty about the future, which means that the ACOL family of models (including the option-value model of Ausink and Wise) is intrinsically incapable of modeling the value of career flexibility. It cannot model the value that Air Force officers place on being able to leave the force at will, and so cannot fully model how Air Force officers will respond to the availability of multiyear contracts, such as those offered under the ACP bonus program.

CHAPTER FOUR

Results of the Dynamic Retention Model

This chapter gives an informal description of the method used to estimate the parameters of the DRM and presents some simulation results for different hypothetical changes to the ACP program. A more formal treatment can be found in Appendix A.

Estimating the Parameters

To estimate the parameters, we model each officer given his or her individual taste for service and a probability distribution over current and future shocks. We assume that officers behave as if they are solving a stochastic, dynamic program to determine whether to stay or leave. Given the taste and shock distributions, we calculate the probability of an officer choosing to stay or leave at each point in time. We then find the parameters for the taste and shock distributions that maximize the likelihood of observing the actual stay-or-leave decisions made by a group of officers.

We draw our data primarily from two sources. Military data come mostly from the Officer Master File and the Officer Loss File for fiscal years (FYs) 1996 through 2001. These data include promotion histories, demographic data, and the retention decisions of individual officers. We also include additional service obligations that accrue from training and promotion, pay and retirement benefits, and promotion rates.

The civilian data come primarily from the Current Population Survey (CPS) 1996 to 2001. These data contain information about civilian earnings and the rate of closure between the pay of retired service members and civilian pay.

As Figure 2.6 implies, we estimate the variance of the shock distribution. The shock distribution is assumed to be normal with mean zero. We also estimate the parameters of the taste distribution, which we assume to be extreme value distributed, as in the original Gotz-McCall model.

Model Estimates

Figure 4.1 provides an example of observed and predicted cumulative retention rates for pilots. It shows a close fit between the observed retention rates and those estimated by the model. The observed retention rates were computed using Kaplan-Meier and are depicted by the circles.

Figure 4.1
Observed and Predicted Pilot Retention Rates

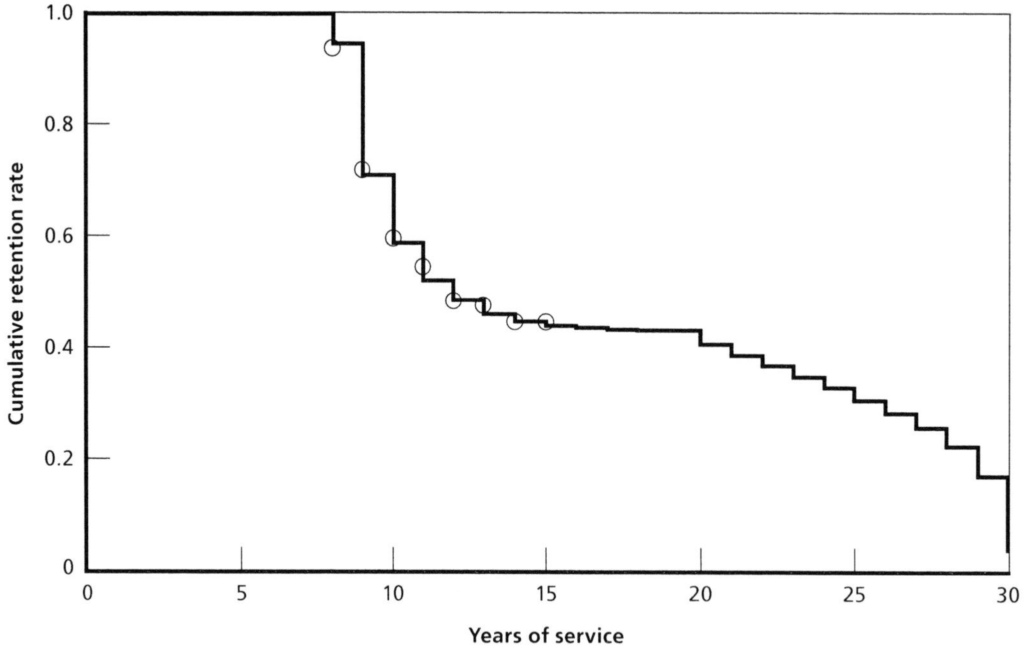

RAND *TR470-4.1*

The step-function shows the predicted retention rate given by the maximum likelihood model estimates.

Figure 4.2 shows the observed versus predicted cumulative retention rate for non-ROTC accessions, and Figure 4.3 shows the predicted versus cumulative retention rates for ROTC accessions. The DRM included indicator values for the mode and scale of the taste distribution for ROTC accessions; the Air Force Academy and other sources of accession were captured by the intercept term for the mode and scale of the taste distribution. The fit to these subgroups is less striking than the overall fit, mainly due to the overprediction of retention for the final two observed years of service (YOS)—YOS 14 and 15—for the non-ROTC accessions. However these final two points account for only 14 of the 1,667 total officers observed.

Simulations Based on the Estimates

The DRM can be used to explore different policy options by taking individual retention decisions and running them through various policy alternatives.

Figure 4.4 depicts the simulated effect of a 10-percent cut in base pay. The left panel shows the change in the cumulative retention rate, with the higher line indicating the baseline retention rates and the lower line showing the effect of the pay cut. The right panel shows the percentage decline in the cumulative retention rate relative to the baseline. The cumulative effect by YOS 15 is to cut retention relative to the baseline by 4 percent. There is little relative decline in retention beyond YOS 15 due to the fact that most of the officers at year 15 and

Figure 4.2
Observed and Predicted Pilot Retention Rates for Non-ROTC Accessions

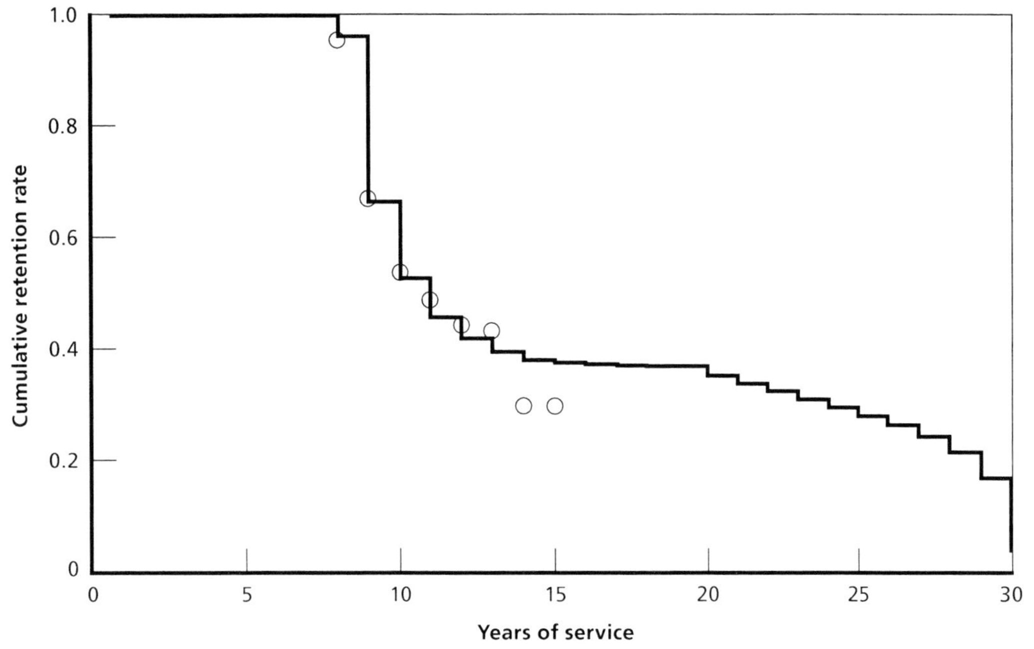

RAND *TR470-4.2*

Figure 4.3
Observed and Predicted Pilot Retention Rates for ROTC Accessions

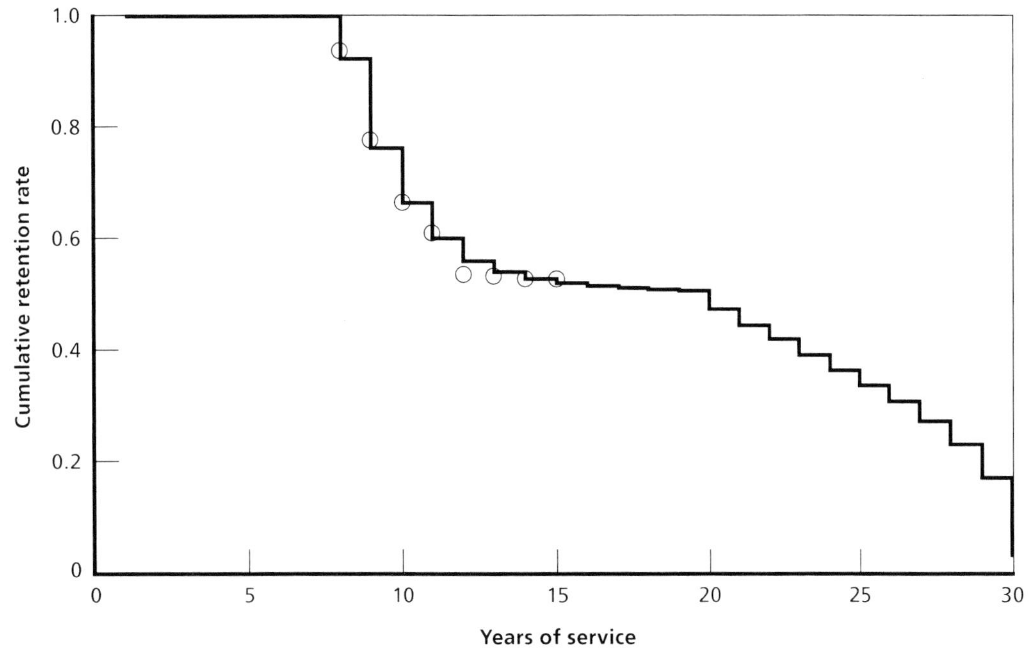

RAND *TR470-4.3*

Figure 4.4
Simulating the Effect of a 10-Percent Pay Cut for Pilots

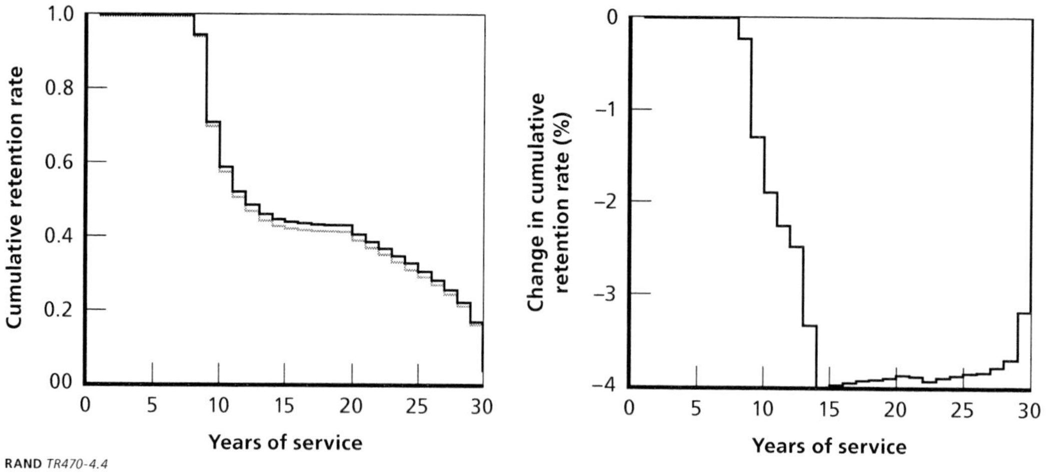

RAND *TR470-4.4*

beyond are participating in the until-20-YAS ACP program.[1] It is important to bear in mind that this simulation compares a baseline to a new regime that has been carried through for all YOS, thus the results for the later YOS should not be interpreted to mean that this is what would happen the first year the change is in place (particularly as most pilots in the Air Force are under contractual obligation to serve until 20 years), but should instead be interpreted as being the steady state the system would evolve to if the change remains in place.

Figure 4.5 shows the results of a more substantive (and more interesting) simulation. It illustrates the kind of analysis that can be done only using the DRM ACP model. Figure 4.5 illustrates the effect of eliminating the until-20-YAS ACP bonus program, while retaining the option for officers to enter into five-year contracts. It shows a decline in retention, which can be attributed to the decline in the cash value of the multiyear contract options. Under the until-20-YAS option, officers can receive up to half of the total bonus pay as an up-front lump sum; this can amount to over $100,000. The elimination of the until-20-YAS option and the associated bonus payment results in a real loss to pilots, which in turn causes a decline in retention rates similar to that seen from a 10-percent pay cut. In this simulation, most of the officers switched from twenty-year contracts to one or more five-year contracts, hence the relatively modest retention effect from the elimination of the 20-year option.[2]

Figure 4.6 shows the simulated results of eliminating the ACP program entirely. It shows a decline in retention of up to 15 percent for the most experienced officers. The average retention effect attributable to ACP over all years implied by this simulation is approximately 7.5 percent for all YOS; this is remarkably close to the estimated effect of ACP on retention reported by Hogan and Espinoza (2003).

---

1 As of FY 2005, the until-20-YAS option is no longer available.

2 As of FY 2005, only initially eligible officers can take the five-year option. There is no longer a five-year extension option.

Figure 4.5
Simulated Effect of Eliminating the 20-Year Option for Pilots

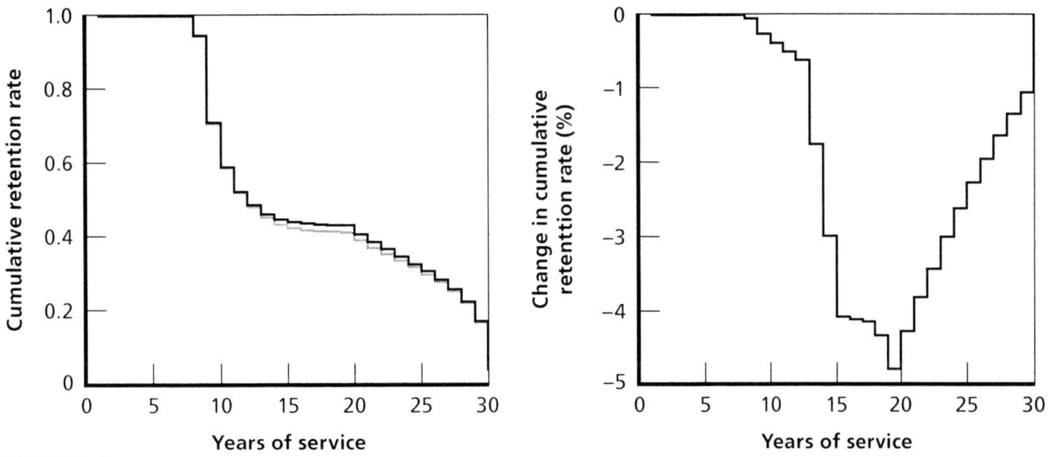

RAND TR470-4.5

Figure 4.6
Simulating Elimination of the ACP Program for Pilots

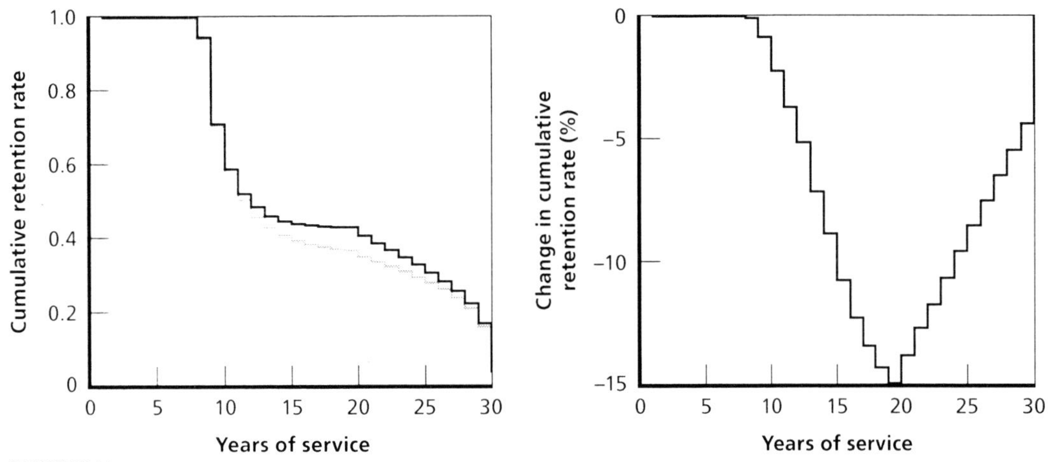

RAND TR470-4.6

Comparison with the Estimates of Gotz and McCall

The parameter estimates the model produces using these data are in some ways qualitatively similar to those developed by Gotz and McCall in 1983.[3] There are also some notable differences. Their model was designed to estimate voluntary retention rates under a broad range of compensation, retirement, and personnel policies. The qualitative similarity of our results to those of Gotz and McCall lends some support to the idea that modeling the individual leads to

[3] Gotz and McCall, 1984.

parameter estimates that are less dependent on the specific structure of policies in effect during the period covered by the data. In particular we find that the mode of the taste distribution is negative, as was found by Gotz and McCall. We also replicate the finding of Gotz and McCall that the estimate of the scale parameter of the taste distribution can be relatively large compared to annual compensation.

Our findings regarding the relationship between the taste distribution of Academy graduates and non-Academy officer accessions differ from those of Gotz and McCall. Specifically, Gotz and McCall found Academy graduates to have lower taste for the military than non-Academy accessions; that is, they were found to have a lower mode parameter for the taste distribution. In addition, Gotz and McCall found Academy graduates to have a smaller scale distribution for their taste distribution. In contrast, we found that Academy graduates and non-Academy accessions did not in general differ significantly in either the mode or the scale of the taste distribution. This difference, while important, comes with a major caveat: In their original work, Gotz and McCall did not present standard errors or confidence intervals for their estimates; therefore, we cannot ascertain whether or not the differences noted in their report were statistically significant.

In addition we found a higher value for the shock term than that found by Gotz and McCall. It is tempting to consider this as preliminary evidence for a genuine change in the magnitude of positive and negative shocks military officers face in these increasingly troubling times.

Conclusions

The DRM fits the data. It offers the Air Force an effective tool for analyzing how officers respond to multiyear agreements. We recommend that the Air Force adopt the DRM and consider widening its application; we have provided computer code and the datasets we used to estimate the models documented in this report to facilitate the wider adoption and application of this model.

APPENDIX A

Implementation Details and Model Estimates

The DRM Model Without ACP

We will begin explaining our approach to implementing the DRM by showing the equations for a simple stay/leave model. This model is very similar to the original Gotz-McCall (1984) model and the later Daula-Moffit model (1995). It omits the Markov promotion process and the selection for reserve versus regular commission present in the original Gotz-McCall model; we will explain why in a later section.

The model consists of two equations, one giving the value of staying for an additional year and revisiting the stay/leave decision and one giving the value of leaving. An officer decides to stay if the value of staying is greater than the value of leaving. To turn this into a statistical model, we add assumptions about the distribution of an independent and identically distributed random shock term and also about the distribution of the officers' taste for military service.

Nonstochastic value of leaving

$$V_t^L = W_t^c + \sum_{\tau=t+1}^{T} \beta^{\tau-t} W_\tau^c + R_t^m$$

Stochastic value of leaving

$$V_t^L + \varepsilon_t^c$$

Where

V_t^L is the value of leaving at time t,

W_t^c is civilian earnings at time t,

$\sum_{\tau=t+1}^{T} \beta^{\tau-t} W_\tau^c$ is the value of future civilian earnings (where β is the annual discount rate),

R_t^m is the retirement benefit accruing to the officer if he or she leaves at time t, and

ε_t^c is random civilian shock at time t.

Nonstochastic value of staying

$$V_t^S = \gamma^m + W_t^m + \beta \ \mathrm{E}_t[\mathrm{Max}(V_{t+1}^L, V_{t+1}^S)]$$

Stochastic value of staying

$$V_t^S + \varepsilon_t^m$$

Where

V_t^S is the value of staying at time *t*,

γ^m is individual taste for the Air Force,

W_t^m is military earnings in the current period *t*,

$\beta \ \mathrm{E}_t[\mathrm{Max}(V_{t+1}^L, V_{t+1}^S)]$ is the discounted expected value of being able to choose to stay or leave in the future, with β being the discount rate, and

ε_t^m is the random military shock at time *t*.

Retention probability in period *t*

$$\begin{aligned}
&\Pr[V_t^S + \varepsilon_t^m > V_t^L + \varepsilon_t^c] \\
&\qquad = \Pr[V_t^S - V_t^L > \varepsilon_t^c - \varepsilon_t^m] \\
&\qquad = \Pr[V_t^S - V_t^L > \varepsilon_t]
\end{aligned}$$

Where

$\varepsilon_t = \varepsilon_t^c - \varepsilon_t^m$ is the difference between the civilian and military shocks at time *t*.

The individual will decide to stay in the military if the value of staying is greater than the value of leaving. If a probability distribution is set for the difference between the random military shock and the random civilian shock, the probability that an individual officer with a particular taste will stay can be computed.

We assume that ε_t is distributed with mean zero and variance σ. This leads to a closed-form solution for the expected value of the maximum of staying or leaving, specifically:

$$\begin{aligned}
\mathrm{E}_t[\mathrm{Max}(V_{t+1}^L, V_{t+1}^S)] &= F((V_{t+1}^S - V_{t+1}^L)/\sigma)V_{t+1}^S \\
&\quad + (1 - F((V_{t+1}^S - V_{t+1}^L)/\sigma))V_{t+1}^L \\
&\quad + f((V_{t+1}^S - V_{t+1}^L)/\sigma)\sigma
\end{aligned}$$

Where

$F(.)$ and $f(.)$ are the cumulative distribution function and probability density function of the unit normal distribution.

In this equation, the first term is the probability of staying multiplied by the value of staying, the second term is the probability of leaving multiplied by the value of leaving, and the third term shows the expected value to the individual of being able to choose whether to stay or leave. This closed-form solution is desirable; otherwise the expected value of the maximum would have to be calculated via numerical integration, which is a relatively slow and imprecise process.

The probability of an individual with taste γ facing shock distribution $F(.)$ choosing to stay in period t can now be computed.

$$\begin{aligned}\Pr[\text{Stay}_t \mid \gamma,\sigma] &= \Pr[\text{Stay}_t] \\ &= \Pr[V_t^S - V_t^L > \varepsilon_t] \\ &= F((V_t^S - V_t^L)/\sigma)\end{aligned}$$

The probability of leaving is simply:

$$\Pr[\text{Leave}_t] = 1 - \Pr[\text{Stay}_t \mid \gamma,\sigma]$$

The following example applies this probability to assess the likelihood of a sequence of events. If we observe a particular individual whose service obligation completed at $t-1$ choosing to stay at $t, t+1$ and leaving at time $t+2$, we can compute the joint probability of this sequence of events like so:

$$\Pr[\text{Stay}_t \mid \gamma,\sigma]\Pr[\text{Stay}_{t+1} \mid \gamma,\sigma]\Pr[\text{Leave}_{t+2} \mid \gamma,\sigma]$$

Similarly, if we observe an individual leaving immediately at the conclusion of his or her service obligation, then the probability is $\Pr[\text{Leave}_t \mid \gamma,\sigma]$. If we observe an individual staying for two periods and then do not observe what they do in the third period, the probability is

$$\Pr[\text{Stay}_t \mid \gamma,\sigma]\Pr[\text{Stay}_{t+1} \mid \gamma,\sigma]$$

In general, the probability of observing someone staying for s periods will be

$$\prod_{\tau=t}^{t+s} \Pr[\text{Stay}_\tau \mid \gamma,\sigma]$$

and the probability of observing someone stay for s periods and then leaving will be

$$(\prod_{\tau=t}^{t+s} \Pr[\text{Stay}_\tau \mid \gamma,\sigma])\Pr[\text{Leave}_{t+s+1} \mid \gamma,\sigma]$$

Of course, this probability is conditioned on the unobservable taste parameter γ. We assume that γ is extreme-value distributed with mode α and scale parameter δ. We will use $g(.)$ to denote the probability density function of this distribution. We can use this distribution to construct an expected probability for a particular sequence of events.

If a person leaves immediately after the conclusion of his or her service obligation at t, the expected value of the probability is

$$L_i(\alpha,\delta,\sigma,\beta) = \int_{-\infty}^{\infty} \Pr[\text{Leave}_t \mid \gamma,\sigma]\, g(\gamma)d\gamma$$

If a person stays for s periods, the expected value will be

$$L_i(\alpha,\delta,\sigma,\beta) = \int_{-\infty}^{\infty} \prod_{\tau=t}^{t+s} \Pr[\text{Stay}_\tau \mid \gamma,\sigma]\, g(\gamma)d\gamma$$

If a person stays for s periods and then leaves, the expected value will be

$$L_i(\alpha,\delta,\sigma,\beta) = \int_{-\infty}^{\infty} \prod_{\tau=t}^{t+s} \Pr[\text{Stay}_\tau \mid \gamma,\sigma]\Pr[\text{Leave}_{t+s+1} \mid \gamma,\sigma]\, g(\gamma)d\gamma$$

Thus the likelihood for the entire sample will be

$$L\ (\alpha,\delta,\sigma,\beta) = \prod_{i=1}^{n} L_i(\alpha,\delta,\sigma,\beta)$$

Modeling a Five-Year Commitment

The model can be expanded to allow the officer the choice to commit for an additional five years. This takes two "stay" equations: one for a one-year commitment that enables an officer to decide on options available at the end of one year and one that allows the officer to decide on options available only at the end of five years.

The nonstochastic value of staying for one period is

$$V_t^{S1} = \gamma^m + W_t^m + \beta\ \mathrm{E}_t[\mathrm{Max}(V_{t+1}^L, V_{t+1}^{S1}, V_{t+1}^{S5})]$$

Where

V_t^{S1} is the value of staying,

γ^m is individual taste for the Air Force,

W_t^m is military earnings in the current year, and

$\beta\ E_t[\mathrm{Max}(V_{t+1}^L, V_{t+1}^{S1}, V_{t+1}^{S5})]$ is the expected value of being able to choose to stay for one year or five years or to leave in the future. β is the annual discount rate.

The nonstochastic value of contracting for five years is captured by the equation

$$V_t^{S5} = \sum_{\tau=t}^{t+4} \beta^{\tau-t}(\gamma^m + W_\tau^{m5}) + \beta^5 E_t[\mathrm{Max}(V_{t+5}^L, V_{t+5}^{S1}, V_{t+5}^{S5})]$$

Where

V_t^{S5} is the value of five-year contract,

$\sum_{\tau=t}^{t+4} \beta^{\tau-t}(\gamma^m + W_\tau^{m5})$ is the discounted present value of military earnings including the bonus for the five-year contract (the W_τ^{m5} term), and

$\beta^5 E_t[\mathrm{Max}(V_{t+5}^L, V_{t+5}^{S1}, V_{t+5}^{S5})]$ is the discounted present value of the expected value of being able to choose to stay for one year or five years or to leave at a point five years in the future.

If an officer makes the decision to stay, he or she is locked in for one or five years, at which time another decision must be made.

We can now compute the probability of an individual with taste γ facing shock distribution $F(.)$ choosing to stay for either one or five years in period t.

$$\begin{aligned}\Pr[\mathrm{Stay}_t \mid \gamma, \sigma] &= \Pr[\mathrm{Max}(V_t^{S1}, V_t^{S5}) - V_t^L > \varepsilon_t] \\ &= F((\mathrm{Max}(V_t^{S1}, V_t^{S5}) - V_t^L) / \sigma)\end{aligned}$$

The probability of leaving is simply

$$\Pr[\mathrm{Leave}_t \mid \gamma, \sigma] = 1 - \Pr[\mathrm{Stay}_t \mid \gamma, \sigma]$$

The construction of the likelihood is a little bit different from that in a model that does not include the possibility of a five-year term. We need to specify the probability of signing up for a one-year term or a five-year term in each period where the officer has a free choice (that is, when he or she is not under a previous commitment to serve five years). The probability of staying one term is

$$\begin{aligned}
&\Pr[\text{Stay}_t^{S1} \mid \gamma,\sigma] \\
&\quad = \Pr[V_t^{S1} - V_t^{L} > \varepsilon_t] = F((V_t^{S1} - V_t^{L}) / \sigma), \quad \text{if } V_t^{S1} \geq V_t^{S5} \\
&\quad = 0, \quad \text{if } V_t^{S1} < V_t^{S5}
\end{aligned}$$

The probability of agreeing to a five-year contract is

$$\begin{aligned}
&\Pr[\text{Stay}_t^{S5} \mid \gamma,\sigma] \\
&\quad = \Pr[V_t^{S5} - V_t^{L} > \varepsilon_t] = F((V_t^{S5} - V_t^{L}) / \sigma), \quad \text{if } V_t^{S1} < V_t^{S5} \\
&\quad = 0, \quad \text{if } V_t^{S1} \geq V_t^{S5}
\end{aligned}$$

Note that the choice of a one-year or a five-year stay is completely determined by the value of an individual's taste parameter and the standard deviation of the shock parameter. There is no random component to the model of the choice of the length of stay. The decision depends on the value of the unobservable taste.

We can now construct the probability of observing a series of stay decisions. If an officer decides to stay for one year and then signs up for a five-year contract, the probability is

$$\Pr[\text{Stay}_t^{S1} \mid \gamma,\sigma] \Pr[\text{Stay}_{t+1}^{S5} \mid \gamma,\sigma]$$

If, on the other hand, an officer is observed to sign up for a five-year obligation and then stays one more year, the probability is

$$\Pr[\text{Stay}_t^{S5} \mid \gamma,\sigma] \Pr[\text{Stay}_{t+5}^{S1} \mid \gamma,\sigma]$$

This construction depends on having data on the five-year contract decision at each decision point. Unfortunately there is no record of participation in the ACP program in the personnel data we use to estimate the model. The data do record whether officers choose to stay or leave during any of the years under observation.

Given that the exact sequence of contract decisions is unknown, we calculate the probability of observing an officer staying a particular number of years (and then leaving or being censored) by summing over all possible sequences of contract decisions. For example, suppose that we observe that an officer stays for two years and then the data are censored. The probability of observing this event is the sum of the probability of one-year stay decision at time t followed by a one-year stay decision at $t + 1$, plus the probability of a one-year stay decision at time t followed by a five-year stay decision at $t + 1$, plus the probability of a five-year stay decision at time t.

Summing over all possible paths is not as bad as it sounds; while the possible number of paths implied by observing, for example, a censored observation of a six-year stay after the end of the initial service obligation is quite large, most of the paths will have near-zero probability. For example, for most values of gamma and sigma the probability of observing a five-year stay decision and then a one-year stay decision is zero. We can exploit this fact in our calculations by noting that if one of the terms in a product is zero, then the entire expression is zero; this saves us having to explicitly calculate the other terms in the expression.

Given this procedure of summing over all the possible paths, the construction of the likelihood for this model is similar to the previous model. For example, suppose that we observe an officer stay for five years after his initial service obligation and then leave. Then the likelihood will be the expected value of the sum over all possible paths (in this case there are only two).

$$\int_{-\infty}^{\infty} (\Pr[\text{Stay}_t^{S5} \mid \gamma,\sigma] \Pr[\text{Leave}_{t+5} \mid \gamma,\sigma] + \prod_{\tau=t}^{t+4} \Pr[\text{Stay}_\tau^{S1} \mid \gamma,\sigma]\, g(\gamma) \Pr[\text{Leave}_{t+5} \mid \gamma,\sigma]\,)d\gamma$$

Terms for the likelihood for other observations are calculated in a similar way.

Modeling the ACP

The most notable historical feature of the ACP program was that officers could agree to a contract where they stayed until 20 YAS.[1] (There is also a 25-YAS option, but for simplicity we do not include it in the model.) The previous model can be expanded to allow the officer the choice to commit to 20 YAS. This requires three "stay" equations: one for a one-year commitment that enables an officer to decide on options available at the end of one year, one that allows the officer to decide on options available only at the end of five years, and one that only allows the officer to decide on options available at the completion of 20 years of aviation service. The system of equations for the behavioral model is similar in structure to the previous model.

The (nonstochastic) value of staying for one period is

$$V_t^{S1} = \gamma + W_t^{m} + \beta\ \mathrm{E}_t[\mathrm{Max}(V_{t+1}^{L}, V_{t+1}^{S1}, V_{t+1}^{S5}, V_{t+1}^{S20})]$$

The (nonstochastic) value of contracting for five years is

$$V_t^{S5} = \sum_{\tau=t}^{t+4} \beta^{\tau-t}(\gamma + W_\tau^{m5}) + \beta^5 \mathrm{E}_t[\mathrm{Max}(V_{t+1}^{L}, V_{t+1}^{S1}, V_{t+1}^{S5}, V_{t+1}^{S20})]$$

---

[1] As of FY 2005, the until-20-YAS option is no longer available.

Note that some of the options may be unavailable at $t + 5$, in which case they are modeled as having zero value.

The (nonstochastic) value of contracting until 20 years of aviation service is

$$V_t^{S20} = \sum_{\tau=t}^{19} \beta^{\tau-t}(\gamma + W_\tau^{m20,t}) + \beta^{20-t} E_t[\text{Max}(V_{20}^L, V_{20}^{S1}, V_{20}^{S5})]$$

The probability of staying becomes

$$\begin{aligned} \Pr[\text{Stay}_t \mid \gamma,\sigma] &= \Pr[\text{Max}(V_t^{S1}, V_t^{S5}, V_t^{S20}) - V_t^L > \varepsilon_t] \\ &= F((\text{Max}(V_t^{S1}, V_t^{S5}, V_t^{S20}) - V_t^L)/\sigma) \end{aligned}$$

The probability of leaving is simply

$$\Pr[\text{Leave}_t \mid \gamma,\sigma] = 1 - \Pr[\text{Stay}_t \mid \gamma,\sigma]$$

The calculation of the probabilities of deciding to stay one year, agreeing to a five-year contract, or agreeing to contract to remain until 20 YAS follows the same logic as was used in the development of the previous model. The creation of the likelihood function, integrating out the individual heterogeneity, follows the same method as outlined in the five-year model.

Challenges Posed in Estimating the Model

Dynamic programming models have a well-deserved reputation for being difficult to use to estimate decisionmaking. The pioneering work of Gotz and McCall did not provide standard errors for the model estimates due to the computing challenges. With the advent of faster computers and improvements in optimization algorithms, the task has become easier, but it is still challenging.

The main challenge is optimizing the likelihood function. Due to the approximation inherent in machine arithmetic, and in particular numerical integration, calculating numerical derivatives is not possible at all points of the likelihood surface. In addition, there seem to be many local maxima—many points on the surface where the gradient will be at or near zero. This means that most hill-climbing algorithms will generally fail.

An additional challenge is posed by the need to integrate out heterogeneity. As there is no closed-form solution for this integral, it has to be estimated numerically. Unfortunately, many modern algorithms for integration, even those that recursively subdivide the interval of integration to a high depth, do not perform well when faced with functions that are near zero over most of the interval. The value of the probability of choosing a five-year contract over a one-year stay or an until-20-YAS contract is one example of a function that is zero for most values of gamma and sigma.

The weak identification of the model parameters also poses a challenge, as it means that straight maximum likelihood estimates of the parameters may veer wildly from values that are credible. The method used in the original work of Gotz and McCall to assure identification is not available to us, as officers were not granted regular or reserve commissions upon entering the officer ranks during the time interval covered by the data. (As a matter of policy, the distinction between reserve commissions and regular commissions will soon disappear entirely; all officers will receive regular commissions.) Gotz and McCall posited that the individuals with higher gamma were more likely to be granted a regular commission. The Gotz and McCall likelihood function used a posterior distribution for gamma that was conditional upon whether or not an officer was granted a regular or reserve commission, the relative proportion of the officers given a reserve commission, and a selectivity parameter that was estimated along with the other model parameters. (In a personal communication to one of the authors in 2002, Glenn Gotz stated that he could not get the original model to converge without adding this selectivity term.)

These challenges are difficult but not insurmountable. Here is one approach that seems to work fairly well.

An Approach to Estimating the Model

In brief, we dealt with the aforementioned challenges using grid search, simulated annealing (the Metropolis algorithm), and Nelder-Mead (the downhill simplex method) to find optima. We used a generalized expectation-maximization (GEM) algorithm for integrating out heterogeneity in some cases.

Typically, researchers use a hill-climbing algorithm to find the values of the parameters of a maximum likelihood estimator (MLE) or maximum a priori (MAP) model. Hill-climbing algorithms do not work well for the ACP version of the DRM, because the model assumes that the decision to make a five-year or an until-20-YAS commitment is dependent on gamma. That is, the model assumes that for each year there is a threshold gamma below which officers would not choose to commit to a five-year contract and would instead choose a one-year contract (if they decided to stay at all). In addition, there is another threshold gamma below which an officer would not choose to take an until-20-YAS contract. The only officers who take the five-year contract in a particular year are those whose gamma falls between the five-year and twenty-year thresholds. This can be a very small interval for some parameter values of the model.

Numerical integration routines sample functions over a finite number of points and estimate the value of the integral based on this sample. If the interval of interest is small, then the numerical integration routine may miss the interval. This means that small parameter changes may result in large changes in the calculated number for the log likelihood (or the MAP figure of merit). These large changes are due to the sample points of the numerical integration routine hitting or missing the possibly small interval. These large changes spell trouble for any hill-climbing algorithm that relies on numerical estimates of the gradient of the likelihood function. Even hill-climbing algorithms that do not rely on estimating the gradient, such as the

Nelder-Mead multidimensional simplex algorithm, can run into trouble, becoming trapped in a local maximum.

This problem can be addressed in two ways. One is to attempt to increase the precision of the numerical integration routine. This is not a particularly effective strategy for the DRM, as simply increasing the number of sample points does not obviate the interaction of the numerical integration routine with the threshold that governs officer behavior in this model. The second way to address this problem, and the technique used in this study, is to use a search algorithm that is well-suited to problems in which there are many local maxima. Simulated annealing (also known as the Metropolis-Hastings algorithm) is one such approach. The simulated annealing algorithm randomly jumps to a point and compares the value of the objective function at the new point with the old best value. With some probability (governed by a Boltzman distribution, for example), it accepts the new point, even if the new point has a lower value for the objective function than the current best point; in this way it avoids getting stuck at a local maximum. As the algorithm progresses, it chooses random points closer and closer to the current best point; it does this according to a "cooling schedule" governed by an optimizer parameter called "temperature." This algorithm bears some resemblance to models of materials undergoing an annealing process, hence the name "simulated annealing."

When the simulated-annealing algorithm found a maximum of the likelihood function, a hill-climbing algorithm (either Nelder-Mead—also known as the downhill simplex method, which is a derivative-free (or Broyden-Fletcher-Goldfarb-Shanno [BFGS]) method, which uses numerical estimates of the gradient) was used to further refine the parameter estimates. Standard errors for the point estimates were calculated using the Berndt-Hall-Hall-Hausman (or "sum of the outer product of the gradients") method.

An Alternative Approach to Estimating the Parameter Values

Some model excursions were estimated using the expectation-maximization (EM) algorithm. This approach avoids the problems caused by the approximate nature of numerical integration noted above. The EM algorithm consists of two steps.[2] In the first step, a likelihood function that depends on the unobservable data (in this case, the individual values of gamma) and assumed values for the rest of the parameters is used to estimate the unobservable data. The second step consists of using the estimated values of the unobservable data in a likelihood function for the complete data model, which is then used to generate estimates of the model parameters. The model parameters generated in the second step are then used as the assumed values in the first step, and the two steps are repeated until the algorithm converges on a set of parameter values.

More formally, we can write the likelihood function for each individual so that it depends on the value of gamma, the individual data x_i, and the model parameters $\theta = (\alpha, \delta, \sigma, \beta)$. For example, if an officer stays for s periods and then leaves, the likelihood would be

[2] Arthur Dempster, Nan Laird, and Donald Rubin, "Maximum Likelihood from Incomplete Data via the EM Algorithm," *Journal of the Royal Statistical Society, Series B (Methodological)*, Vol. 39, No. 1, 1977, pp. 1–38.

$$L_i(\gamma_i \mid x_i,\theta) = \prod_{\tau=t}^{t+s} \Pr[\text{Stay}_\tau \mid \gamma_i, x_i, \theta] \Pr[\text{Leave}_{t+s+1} \mid \gamma_i, x_i, \theta]\, g(\gamma \mid \theta)$$

Step 1. Find the value of γ_i that maximizes the individual likelihood, assuming that the parameter vector is $\hat{\theta}^0$:

$$\hat{\gamma}_i^{\,1} = \arg\max_{\gamma_i} L_i(\gamma_i \mid x_i, \hat{\theta}^0)$$

Step 2. Find the value of θ that maximizes the individual likelihood given the values for the individual gammas estimated in step 1 and the data:

$$\hat{\theta}^1 = \arg\max_{\theta} L(\hat{\gamma}^1 \mid x, \hat{\theta}^1)$$

Then iterate over the two steps, substituting the nth estimate of θ into the $(n+1)$th iteration of step 1 to estimate

$$\hat{\gamma}_i^{\,n+1} = \arg\max_{\gamma_i} L_i(\gamma_i \mid x_i, \hat{\theta}^n)$$

and then use the new estimates of γ_i to generate new estimates of

$$\hat{\theta}^{n+1} = \arg\max_{\theta} L(\hat{\gamma}^{n+1} \mid x, \hat{\theta}^n)$$

until the algorithm converges on a value of $\hat{\theta}$.

This algorithm generally converges to the maximum likelihood solution; convergence is not guaranteed, however. EM can be applied to MAP estimation as well as MLE; the MAP objective function is simply substituted for the likelihood function in step 2.

This algorithm has been generalized to the case where in each step values of the unobservable data and the parameters of the full data model are chosen that merely improve the likelihood function.[3] If each step assures some improvement, then the algorithm can be shown to have similar convergence properties to an algorithm using the optimal values of the unobserved data and the model parameters. This is the GEM algorithm.

The GEM algorithm is very useful for estimating models with unobserved individual heterogeneity. As can be seen from the description above, it avoids the need to integrate out heterogeneity. This leads to a significant reduction in the computer time needed to estimate models

---

[3] Radford Neal and Geoffrey Hinton, "A View of the EM Algorithm That Justifies Incremental, Sparse, and Other Variants," in Michael I. Jordan, ed., *Learning in Graphical Models*, Cambridge, Mass.: MIT Press, 1999, pp. 355–368.

with unobserved individual heterogeneity and facilitates exploration of additional sources of heterogeneity (e.g., in the individual discount rate for future earnings). We used this approach to explore alternative models, including indicator variables for race and gender as regressors for the parameters of the taste distribution.

Details of the Computer Implementation

We have included complete listings of the datasets used along with sample computer code as an aid to readers interested in replicating the work discussed here or in extending or improving this model of officer behavior. The listings should help in clearing up any ambiguity in the mathematical description of the model given above. Hopefully, this will save future workers in this arena much wasted time and effort. The code shown is perhaps not the most efficient or elegant; it was designed with an eye toward assuring correctness rather than maximizing efficiency. We will now discuss some of the details of our implementation of the model.

The estimation program is implemented in R, a computer language and environment for statistical computing.[4] This free software is distributed under the terms of the GNU GENERAL PUBLIC LICENSE Version 2, June 1991. It is available in both source and binary versions for a wide variety of computer platforms. R is used by many working statisticians; many papers in statistics now feature snippets of R code as a way of communicating research methods. The user interface for the implementation of R on the Microsoft Windows® operating system is illustrated in Figure A.1. The figure shows the user console in the right panel, depicting the progress of the estimation routine, and shows plots of the current best model estimates of the cumulative continuation rate: The lower plot gives the rate for ROTC accessions, and the upper plot gives the rate for

Figure A.1
R Implementation of the ACP DRM

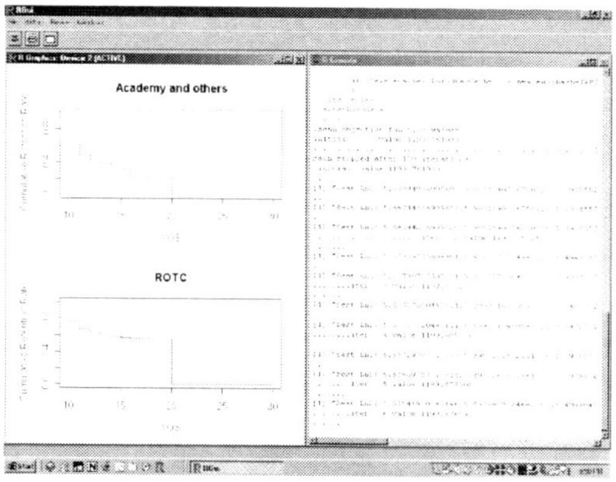

RAND *TR470-A.1*

[4] R Development Core Team, *R: A Language and Environment for Statistical Computing*, computer language, Vienna, Austria: R Foundation for Statistical Computing, 2005.

Air Force Academy accessions. These graphics are very useful for diagnosing model fit problems, and we strongly recommend the use of graphical output in this context.

As in most dynamic programming models, the vast majority of the time that a computer needs to run the DRM is spent calculating the value functions. The value functions are calculated covering a span of up to 25 years (for the case where an officer has a five-year initial service obligation and could possibly stay for up to 30 years). The value function is computed recursively. The implementation caches the intermediate results of the recursive computation of the value functions, resulting in a substantial reduction in the time needed to compute the value functions. Without caching, the program would repeatedly solve many identical subproblems; by caching, the program solves a subproblem only once and stores the computed value in the cache, and repeated calls to the function result in the program pulling the value from the cache rather than recomputing the result from scratch. Specifically, we cache the function that calculates the expected value of the maximum; caching only this function is sufficient to gain most of the benefits to be gained from caching. Other intermediate values are also cached, as appropriate.

This program uses the R **optim()** function to maximize the MLE objective function, using the R implementations of simulated annealing, Nelder-Mead, and BFGS where appropriate.

Estimates

The estimates produced by the DRM include estimates of the parameters of the shock distribution and the taste distribution and estimates of the coefficients on indicator variables for gender and race. The estimated shock distribution is the difference of the civilian and the military shock distribution. The shock distribution is assumed to be normal with mean zero, so the only parameter estimated for the shock distribution is the variance. The taste distribution is assumed to be an extreme value distribution, which is parameterized by a mode and scale parameter. In the case where different estimates of the taste distribution are made by the source of accession, the omitted group is the set of officers not accessed from ROTC, and indicator variables are used to estimate differences in the mode and scale parameter for accessions from ROTC.

We attempted to estimate the parameters by occupation, modeling the following categories: pilots, other rated officers, operational officers other than pilots, and mission support officers. Only two occupations, pilots and mission support, had sufficient sample sizes (>1,000) to allow the model to produce valid estimates. The results for each are shown in Table A.1 and Table A.2, respectively.

The estimates reported below assume promotion to be deterministic; this is similar to the approach used by Daula and Moffitt (1995). This differs from the original Gotz-McCall model, which used a sophisticated Markov model of promotion that took into account both the grade and the YOS when an officer was promoted into a grade. This technique allows for differing qualities of officers; for example, it would allow for officers that were promoted more rapidly to captain to be more rapidly promoted to major. An earlier version of the model used the same approach to model promotion, but was abandoned due to difficulties in getting the

Table A.1
MLE Estimates for Pilot ACP DRM

		par	s.e.	z	P[|z|>0]
90th percentile wage					
N	1,667				
–1*log likelihood	1,758.40				
ln(-alpha) mode of taste		4.97	1.26	3.95	1.00
ln(delta) scale of taste		5.40	1.31	4.14	1.00
ln(sigma) s.d. of shock		6.34	1.05	6.04	1.00
ln(–alpha2) source==ROTC		–1.71	0.47	–3.61	1.00
ln(delta2) source==ROTC		–0.48	0.56	–0.86	0.80
beta		0.90			
Median pilot wage					
N	1,667				
–1*log likelihood	1,770.21				
ln(–alpha) mode of taste		4.14	0.53	7.85	1.00
ln(delta) scale of taste		3.29	1.76	1.87	0.97
ln(sigma) s.d. of shock		5.90	0.40	14.58	1.00
ln(–alpha2) source==ROTC		–0.17	0.37	–0.45	0.67
ln(delta2) source==ROTC		0.46	1.30	0.36	0.64
beta		0.90			
90th percentile wage					
N	1,667				
–1*log likelihood	1,762.25				
ln(–alpha) mode of taste		4.44	2.00	2.22	0.99
ln(delta) scale of taste		4.81	1.85	2.60	1.00
ln(sigma) s.d. of shock		6.08	1.55	3.91	1.00
ln(–alpha2) source==ROTC		–1.90	1.79	–1.06	0.86
ln(delta2) source==ROTC		0.01	0.69	0.02	0.51
beta		0.85			
Median pilot wage					
N	1,667				
–1*log likelihood	1,762.05				

Table A.1—Continued

	par	s.e.	z	P[|z|>0]
ln(–alpha) mode of taste	5.16	1.66	3.11	1.00
ln(delta) scale of taste	5.72	1.87	3.07	1.00
ln(sigma) s.d. of shock	6.45	1.69	3.83	1.00
ln(–alpha2) source==ROTC	–1.97	1.14	–1.73	0.96
ln(delta2) source==ROTC	–0.50	0.46	–1.08	0.86
beta	0.85			

Table A.2
MLE Estimates for Mission Support Officers

		par	s.e.	z	P[|z|>0]
50th percentile wage					
N	958				
–1*log likelihood	1,289.40				
ln(–alpha) mode of taste		2.83	0.76	3.74	1.00
ln(delta) scale of taste		3.12	3.59	0.87	0.81
ln(sigma) s.d. of shock		5.90	1.42	4.16	1.00
ln(–alpha2) source==ROTC		–6.93	1,593.72	0.00	0.50
ln(delta2) source==ROTC		–0.77	8.28	–0.09	0.54
beta		0.90			
50th percentile wage					
N	958				
–1*log likelihood	1,283.97				
ln(–alpha) mode of taste		–4.20	1,281.91	0.00	0.50
ln(delta) scale of taste		1.76	8.38	0.21	0.58
ln(sigma) s.d. of shock		5.23	1.16	4.52	1.00
ln(–alpha2) source==ROTC		7.83	1,282.27	0.01	0.50
ln(delta2) source==ROTC		1.97	7.12	0.28	0.61
beta		0.85			

maximum likelihood model to converge. This is likely due to the fact that in the dataset under consideration, there was little variance in officer promotion timings and no observed correlation in sequential promotion timings (that is, a below-the-zone promotion in lower ranks was not a significant predictor of a below-the-zone promotion in higher ranks).

The estimates reported below assume values for the discount parameter beta. We took this approach because the parameter beta is only weakly identified in the model, and we found that attempting to estimate beta along with the other parameter values resulted in a large increase in computation time while the estimated betas varied little from the assumed starting values. The value of beta is assumed to be either 0.85 or 0.90.

The estimates reported for pilots assume that the civilian pilot wage corresponds either to the 90th percentile of all wages observed or to the 50th percentile of all pilot wages observed in the civilian population. While the differing assumptions result in different estimates for the taste distribution, the differing parameter estimates had little impact on model fit or on the corresponding simulations.

The estimates reported for mission support officers assume that the civilian wage corresponds to the 50th percentile of all wages observed in the civilian population of full-time workers. We also made estimates assuming that the civilian wage corresponds to the 75th percentile of all wages observed; however, these estimates did not fit the data as well as the ones made using the 50th percentile assumption. Figure A.2 shows the model fit for the first set of coefficients reported in Table A.2.

Figure A.2
Observed and Predicted Retention Rates for Mission Support Officers (DRM)

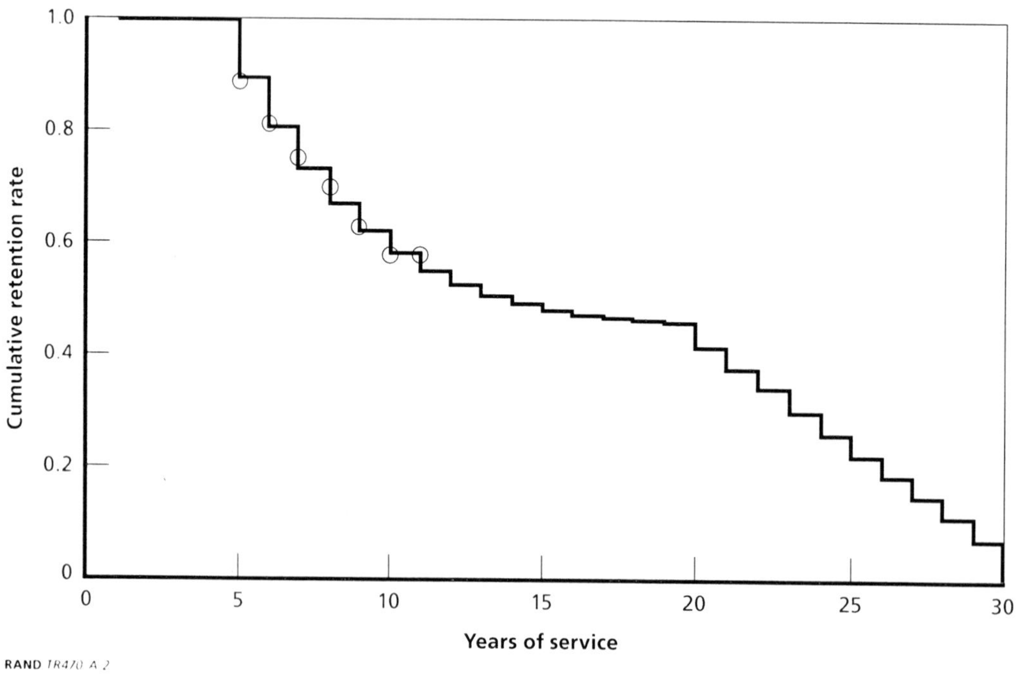

RAND TR470 A.2

Comparing DRM and ACOL 2 Model Performance

The most commonly used model for studying Air Force officer retention is ACOL 2. Figures A.3 and A.4 show the fit of the DRM and ACOL 2 model to the data for pilots used in this study, and Figures A.5 to A.9 show simulation results for both models. Much the same code that was used to produce the estimates using the DRM was also used to create the estimates generated by the ACOL 2 model, the only difference being the expression giving the expected value of the maximum in the DRM was replaced by an expression giving the maximum of the

Figure A.3
DRM and ACOL 2 Predicted Cumulative Retention Rates for Pilots

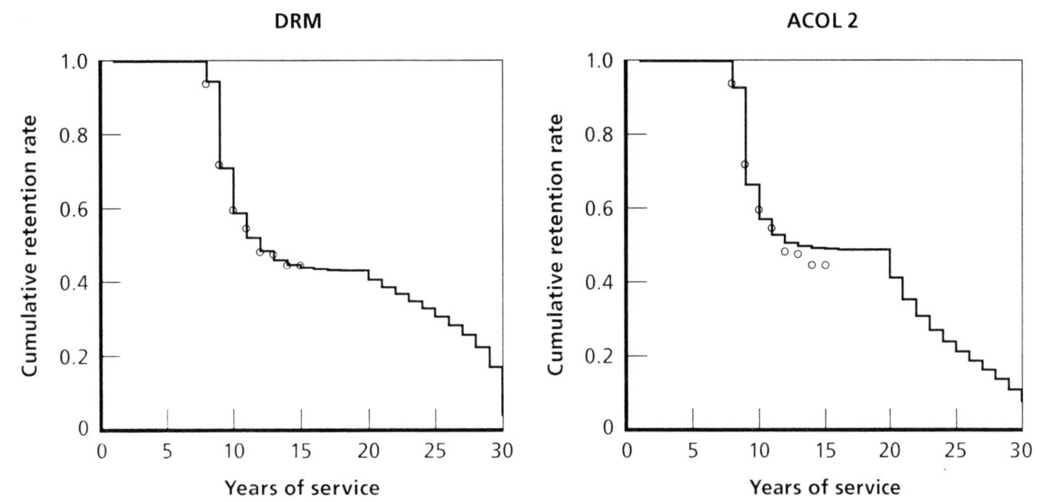

Figure A.4
DRM and ACOL 2 Predicted-Actual Cumulative Continuation Rates for Pilots

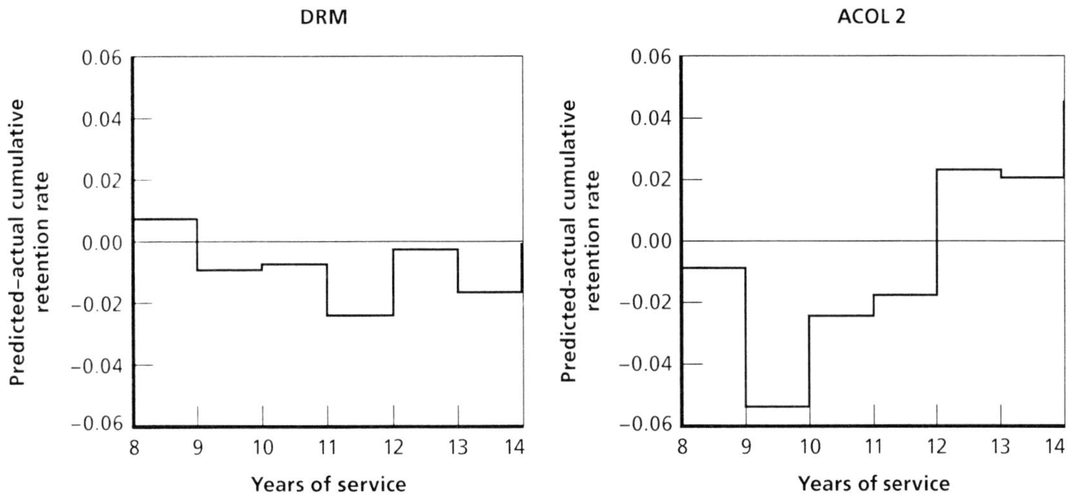

expected values in the ACOL 2 model. Note that the resulting ACOL 2 model is slightly different from most ACOL 2 models currently in use, due to differing assumptions regarding the distribution of taste (extreme-value rather than normal) and regarding the distribution of the shock term (normal rather than extreme-value). Thus, the difference in model performance is due solely to the differing ways in which the value of future choices is modeled.

The fit of the models to pilot data can be seen in Figure A.3 and Figure A.4. In these figures, as in all the figures below, the DRM run is shown on the left and the corresponding ACOL 2 model run is shown on the right. The first thing to note is that the DRM provides a closer fit to the observed cumulative retention rates than the ACOL 2 model. The DRM provides a fairly close fit throughout the observed range, whereas the ACOL 2 systematically underpredicts early-year retention and overpredicts later-year retention.

The difference between the two models becomes more evident in the simulations. In the first simulation, a 10-percent pay cut, the DRM simulation shows up to a 4-percent change in the cumulative continuation rate (see Figure A.5). The ACOL 2 simulation shows barely any response to the pay cut; the predicted change in officer retention is less than the line thickness of the graph. For the remaining simulations, however, the results are quite different (see Figure A.6 and Figure A.7). The simulated response under the ACOL 2 model is considerably larger than the response under the DRM. In fact, the simulated response under the ACOL 2 model is so large as to be not credible.

What accounts for the ACOL 2 model's lack of responsiveness to a small change in compensation and its over-responsiveness to a substantive change in the ACP program? They are at least in part caused by the very nature of the ACOL 2 model: It does not correctly calculate the effect of option values. Given the ACOL 2 behavioral assumptions, only those changes that will affect the expected optimal leaving time, or largely impact those years before the expected optimal leaving time, will show significant behavioral impacts. This is the commonly used

Figure A.5
DRM and ACOL Simulations of the Effect of a 10-Percent Pay Cut for Pilots

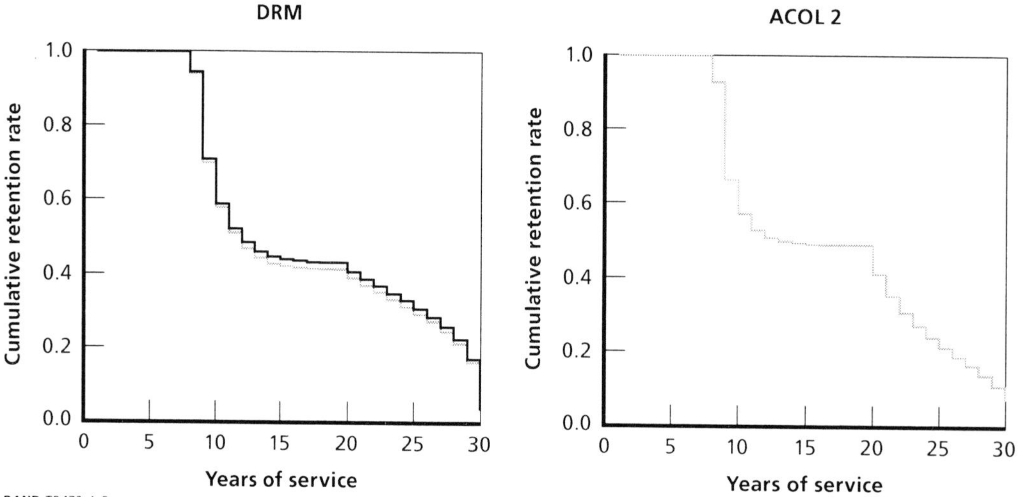

RAND *TR470-A.5*

Figure A.6
DRM and ACOL Simulations of the Effect of Eliminating the 20-Year Option for Pilots

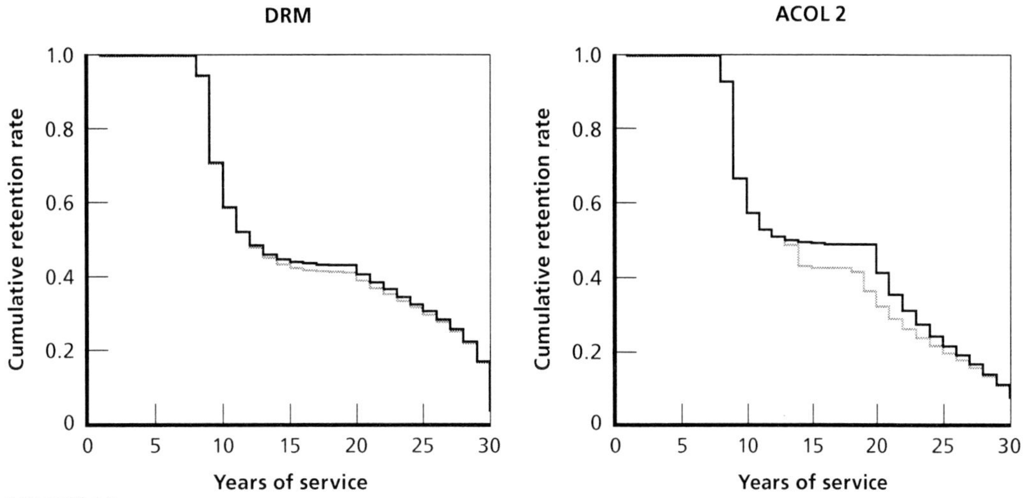

RAND *TR470-A.6*

Figure A.7
DRM and ACOL Simulations of the Effect of Eliminating ACP for Pilots

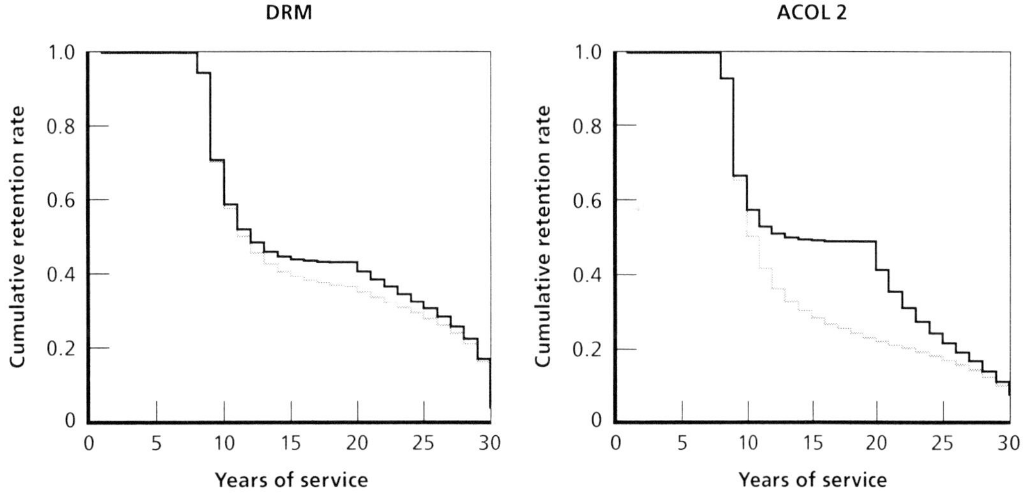

RAND *TR470-A.7*

justification for not using ACOL 2 to study the impact of retirement reforms. In this case, the simulated pay cut is too small to change the expected optimal leaving time (because of the heavy role that ACP plays in retention decisions), while the changes to the ACP have a direct impact on the expected optimal leaving time.

We hasten to add that this is merely one example of the difference in the performance of the ACOL 2 model and the DRM. While this one example cannot provide definitive proof of the superiority of one approach vis-à-vis the other, it definitely provides food for thought for those researchers who are considering relying on ACOL 2 in their future efforts, particularly those cases where the value that individuals place on future options plays an important part in those individuals' decision calculus.

In cases where option values play a less important role, continued used of the ACOL 2 model may be justified. Consider, for example, the fit performance of both models for the data for mission support officers shown in Figure A.8. For all intents and purposes the model fit is identical. However, as Figure A.9 illustrates, it is important to note that similar fit does not

Figure A.8
DRM and ACOL 2 Predicted Cumulative Retention Rates for Mission Support Officers

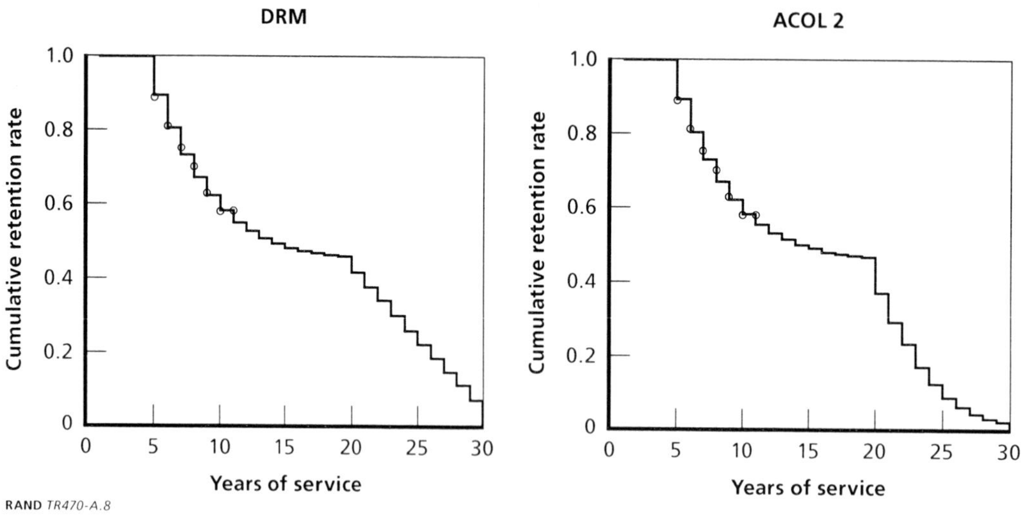

Figure A.9
DRM and ACOL Simulations of the Effect of 10-Percent Pay Cut for Mission Support Officers

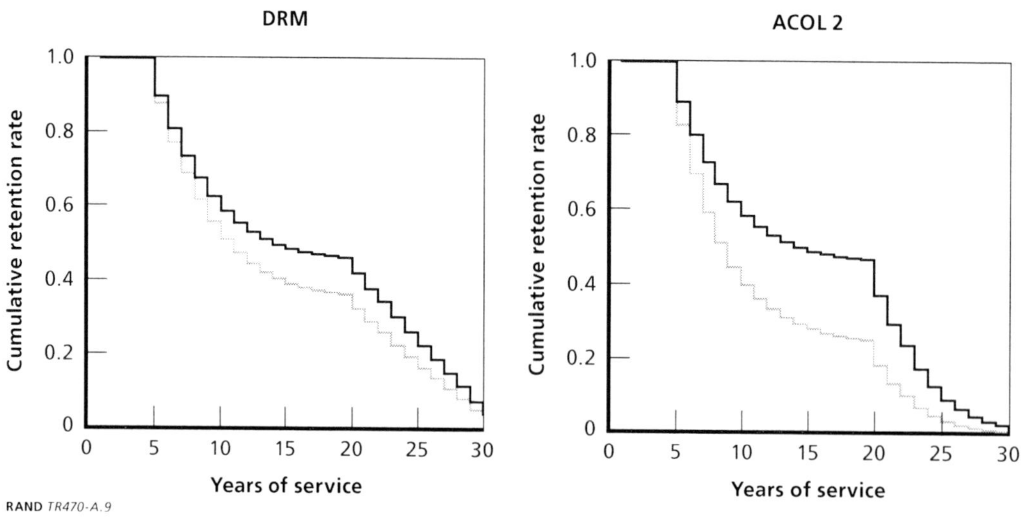

guarantee similar results when simulating a policy option. Figure A.9 shows that the simulated effect of a 10-percent pay cut for mission support officers is highly dependent on the model chosen. Again, the simulation results from the DRM seem more credible.

APPENDIX B

Computer Program and Data

Listing 1—Dynamic Retention Model with ACP

```
#	Dynamic Retention Model with Extensions for ACP
#	Michael G. Mattock, RAND Corporation, 2006
#	http://www.rand.org
#

#	This is an implementation of the Dynamic Retention Model by Glen Gotz and
#	John McCall, extended to cover the Aviator Continuation Pay program by
#	Michael G. Mattock.

#
#	Numerical integration routine relies on the gauss.quad function of the
#	"statmod" package available at http://cran.r-project.org.
#

#	Quantile and density function for the extreme value distribution

qev <- function(x, alpha, delta) { alpha - delta*log(log(1/x)) }

dev <- function(x, alpha, delta) { exp(-exp((alpha - x)/delta) + (alpha - x)/delta)/delta }

#	Mean military wages by year of service for Air Force Officers, excluding ACP
bonuses

militarywages <- c(38192, 38192, 48519, 53849, 62372, 62577, 64811, 64811, 67308, 67308, 69438,
74101, 82664, 82664, 84880, 84880, 90175, 96787, 98795, 98795, 100754, 100754, 114150, 115748,
117970, 117970, 122279, 122279, 126747, 141565, 141565, 141789, 155703, 155703, 155703, 155703,
161849, 168332, 168332, 171810, 175852)
```

```
militarywages <- militarywages/1000

Wm <- function(t) { militarywages[t] }

#       Wages by year of experience for civilian population

percentile50th <- c(25.96735, 28.20255, 30.52769, 32.89876, 35.27562, 37.62200, 39.90547,
42.09747, 44.17330, 46.11210, 47.89691, 49.51458, 50.95586, 52.21534, 53.29146, 54.18656, 54.90678,
55.46218, 55.86662, 56.13788, 56.29754, 56.37109, 56.38785, 56.38100, 56.38760, 56.44854, 56.60860,
56.91639, 57.42441, 58.18898)

percentile90th <- c(44.04211, 51.16259, 58.10669, 64.80436, 71.19354, 77.22015, 82.83808,
88.00922, 92.70344, 96.89858, 100.58048, 103.74296, 106.38780, 108.52480, 110.17171, 111.35428,
112.10625, 112.46931, 112.49318, 112.23552, 111.76201, 111.14627, 110.46994, 109.82263, 109.30193,
109.01342, 109.07065, 109.59517, 110.71649, 112.57214)

pilotwages <- c(33137, 37504, 41694, 45705, 49537, 53191, 56667, 59964, 63083, 66023, 68785,
71369, 73774, 76000, 78049, 79918, 81610, 83122, 84457, 85613, 86590, 87389, 88010, 88452, 88716,
88801, 88708, 88437, 87987, 87358, 86551, 85566, 84402, 83060, 81540, 79841, 77963, 75907, 73673,
71260)
pilotwages <- pilotwages/1000

# Wc <- function(t) { pilotwages[t] }

Wc <- function(t) { percentile90th[t] }

#       Bonus payments

bonus5 <- 20
bonus20prime <- 25

#       The Air Force allows officers who sign up for the until-20-years option
#       to receive up to half of the projected stream of bonus payments as an
#       up-front lump-sum payment. This payment is capped at 150,000 dollars.

AdvancePaymentLimit <- 150

bonus20 <- function(year,commitment){
        if (year > commitment) return(0)

        else if (year==1){
                min(AdvancePaymentLimit,(bonus20prime*commitment)/2)
        } else {
```

```
            ( (bonus20prime*commitment)-min(AdvancePaymentLimit,(bonus20prime*commitment)
/2) )/(commitment-1)
        }
}

#       The time horizon is limited to thirty years of service.

T <- 30


#
#       VS1 calculates the value of staying one additional year
#

VS1 <- function(gamma, sigma, beta, t) {
        if (t>=T+1){
                value <- 0
        } else {
                value <- gamma + Wm(t) + (beta)*EV(gamma, sigma, beta, t+1)
        }
        value
}

#
#       VS5 calculates the value of staying five additional years
#

LastYearEligible5 <- 15

VS5 <- function(gamma, sigma, beta, t) {
        if (t>LastYearEligible5){
                value <- 0
        } else {
                value <- 0
                for(i in 0:4){
                        value <- value + ((beta)^(i))*(Wm(t+i) + gamma + bonus5)
                }
                value <- value + (beta^(5))*EV(gamma, sigma, beta, t+5)
        }
        value
}

#
```

```
#       VS20 calculates the value of staying until 20 YOS
#

LastYearEligible20 <- 14
VestingYear <- 20

VS20 <- function(gamma, sigma, beta, t) {
        if (t>LastYearEligible20){
                value <- 0
        } else {
                commitment <- VestingYear - t
                value <- 0
                for(s in 0:(VestingYear-t-1)){
                        value <- value + ((beta)^s)*(Wm(t+s) + gamma + bonus20(s+1,commitment))
                }
                value <- value + (beta^(VestingYear-t))*EV(gamma, sigma, beta, (VestingYear))
        }
        value
}



#
#       R calculates the value of the DPV stream of payments from military retirement
under cliff vesting
#


R <- function(t, beta){
        if (t>=VestingYear) {
                temp <- Wm(t)
                (1/(1-beta))*((temp/2)+((t-VestingYear)/10)*(temp/4))
        } else {
                0
        }
}

#
#       VL calculates the value of leaving, and caches its results in VLCache
#
VLCache <- new.env(hash=FALSE)

VL <- function(gamma, sigma, beta, t) {
```

```
        name <- paste("VL", beta, t)
        if (exists(name, env=VLCache)) return(get(name, env=VLCache)) else
        if (t>=T+1) {
                value <- 0
        } else {
                value <- 0
                for (s in t:T) {
                        value <- value + beta^(s-t)*Wc(s)
                }
                value <- value + R(t, beta)
        }
        assign(name, value, VLCache)
        value
}

#
#       EV calculates the expected value of the maximum of staying or leaving
#       EV chaches its results in EVCache
#

EVCache <- new.env(hash=TRUE)

EV <- function(gamma, sigma, beta, t) {
        name <- paste("EV", gamma, sigma, beta, t)
        vs1x <- VS1(gamma, sigma, beta, t)
        fn1 <- function(vs){
                vl <- VL(gamma, sigma, beta, t)
                a <- vs - vl
                F <- pnorm(a/sigma)
                F*vs + (1-F)*vl + sigma*dnorm(a/sigma)
        }

        if(t<=LastYearEligible20) {
                vs20x <- VS20(gamma, sigma, beta, t)
                if (t<=LastYearEligible5) {
                        vs5x <- VS5(gamma, sigma, beta, t)
                        if (!is.na((vs20x>max(vs5x,vs1x)))&(vs20x>max(vs5x,vs1x))){
                                value <- fn1(vs20x)
                        } else if (!is.na((vs5x>vs1x))& (vs5x>vs1x)){
                                value <- fn1(vs5x)
                        } else {
                                value <- fn1(vs1x)
                        }
```

```
            } else {
                    ifelse( (!is.na((vs20x>vs1x))& (vs20x>vs1x)), value <- fn1(vs20x), value
<- fn1(vs1x))
            }

        } else {
            if (t<=LastYearEligible5) {
                    vs5x <- VS5(gamma, sigma, beta, t)
                    ifelse( (!is.na((vs5x>vs1x))& (vs5x>vs1x)), value <- fn1(vs5x), value
<- fn1(vs1x))
            } else {
                    value <- fn1(vs1x)
            }
        }
        assign(name, value, EVCache)
        value
}



#
#       PrStay calculates the probability of staying in period t
#


PrStay <- function(gamma, sigma, beta, t) {
        sum(PrStayAll(gamma, sigma, beta, t))
}


#
#       PrStay1 calculates the probability of staying for 1 period in period t
#

PrStay1 <- function(gamma, sigma, beta, t) PrStayAll(gamma, sigma, beta, t)[1]


#
#       PrStay5 calculates the probability of signing on to a 5-year contract
#

PrStay5 <- function(gamma, sigma, beta, t) PrStayAll(gamma, sigma, beta, t)[2]
```

```
#
#       PrStay20 calculates the probability of signing on to an until-20-years
#       contract.
#

PrStay20 <- function(gamma, sigma, beta, t) PrStayAll(gamma, sigma, beta, t)[3]

#
#       PrStayAll computes the probabilities for all lengths of stay
#


PrStayCache <- new.env(hash=TRUE)

PrStayAll <- function(gamma, sigma, beta, t) {
        name <- paste("PrStay", gamma, sigma, beta, t)
        if (exists(name, env=PrStayCache)) return(get(name, env=PrStayCache)) else

        vs1x <- VS1(gamma, sigma, beta, t)
        fn1 <- function(vs){
                vl <- VL(gamma, sigma, beta, t)
                pnorm((vs-vl)/sigma)
        }

        if(t<=LastYearEligible20) {
                vs20x <- VS20(gamma, sigma, beta, t)
                if (t<=LastYearEligible5) {
                        vs5x <- VS5(gamma, sigma, beta, t)
                        if (!is.na((vs20x>max(vs5x,vs1x)))&(vs20x>max(vs5x,vs1x))){
                                value <- c(0,0,fn1(vs20x))
                        } else ifelse((!is.na((vs5x>vs1x))& (vs5x>vs1x)),value <-
c(0,fn1(vs5x),0),value <- c(fn1(vs1x),0,0))
                } else {
                        ifelse( (!is.na((vs20x>vs1x))& (vs20x>vs1x)), value <- c(0,0,fn1(vs20x)),
value <- c(fn1(vs1x),0,0))
                }
        } else {
                if (t<=LastYearEligible5) {
                        vs5x <- VS5(gamma, sigma, beta, t)
                        ifelse( (!is.na((vs5x>vs1x))& (vs5x>vs1x)), value <- c(0,fn1(vs5x),0),
value <- c(fn1(vs1x),0,0))
                } else {
```

```
                    value <- c(fn1(vs1x),0,0)
            }
        }
        assign(name, value, PrStayCache)
        value
}


#
#       Lnf1 calculates the probability of of observing the sequence of states given by the
the vector obs, for a given taste gamma
#

Lnf1 <- function(gamma, sigma, beta, states, liso) {
        pr <- 1
        for (s in 1:(length(states))) {
                if (states[s] > 5) {
                        pr <- pr*PrStay20(gamma, sigma, beta, (sum(states[1:s])-states[s]+liso))
                } else if (states[s] == 5){
                        pr <- pr*PrStay5(gamma, sigma, beta, (sum(states[1:s])-states[s]+liso))
                } else if (states[s] == 1){
                        pr <- pr*PrStay1(gamma, sigma, beta, (sum(states[1:s])-states[s]+liso))
                } else if (states[s] == 0){
                        pr <- pr*(1-PrStay(gamma, sigma, beta, (sum(states[1:
s])-states[s]+liso)))
                }
                test = (pr==0)
                if (is.na(test)) pr <- 0
                if (pr==0) break
        }
        pr
}

#
#       get _ state _ vectors _ stay and get _ state _ vectors _ leave compute all possible
#       paths corresponding to an observed sequence of stay and/or leave events
#


get _ state _ vectors _ stay <- function(state _ vector, tau, liso){
        if (sum(state _ vector) >= tau+1) {
                return(list(state _ vector))
        } else if (sum(state _ vector)+liso <= LastYearEligible20){
```

```
                c(get_state_vectors_stay(c(state_vector, VestingYear-(sum(state_
vector)+liso)), tau, liso), get_state_vectors_stay(c(state_vector, 5), tau, liso), get_
state_vectors_stay(c(state_vector, 1), tau, liso))
        } else if (sum(state_vector)+liso <= LastYearEligible5){
                c(get_state_vectors_stay(c(state_vector, 5), tau, liso), get_state_
vectors_stay(c(state_vector, 1), tau, liso))
        } else {
                c(get_state_vectors_stay(c(state_vector, 1), tau, liso))
        }
}

get_state_vectors_leave <- function(state_vector, tau, liso){
        if (tau == 0) {
                return(list(c(0)))
        } else if (sum(state_vector) == tau) {
                return(list(c(state_vector, 0)))
        } else if ((VestingYear-liso <= tau)&(sum(state_vector)+liso <= LastYearEligible20)){
                c(get_state_vectors_leave(c(state_vector, VestingYear-(sum(state_
vector)+liso)), tau, liso), get_state_vectors_leave(c(state_vector, 5), tau, liso), get_
state_vectors_leave(c(state_vector, 1), tau, liso))
        } else if ((sum(state_vector)+5 <= tau)&(sum(state_vector)+liso <=
LastYearEligible5)){
                c(get_state_vectors_leave(c(state_vector, 5), tau, liso), get_state_
vectors_leave(c(state_vector, 1), tau, liso))
        } else {
                c(get_state_vectors_leave(c(state_vector, 1), tau, liso))
        }
}

#
#       Lnf3_stay and Lnf3_leave compute the probability of observing a particular
#       sequence of events, integrating out heterogeneity.
#

Lnf3StayCache <- new.env(hash=TRUE)

Lnf3_stay <- function(alpha, delta, sigma, beta, tau, liso) {
        name <- paste("Stay", alpha, delta, sigma, beta, tau, liso)
        if (exists(name, env=Lnf3StayCache )){
#               cat("+")
#               flush.console()
                return(get(name,env=Lnf3StayCache ))
        } else {
```

```
#               cat(".")
#               flush.console()



        z <- get_state_vectors_stay(c(),tau,liso)
        fn1 <- function(gamma) {

                fn0 <- function(states) {
                        Lnf1(gamma, sigma, beta, states, liso)
                }
                dev(gamma, alpha, delta)*sum(sapply(z,fn0))
        }

 lo <- qev(0.0005, alpha, delta)
        up <- qev(0.9995, alpha, delta)

        value <- nintegrate(fn1, lo, up)

        assign(name,value,Lnf3StayCache)
#       print(paste("Stay", "tau =", tau, "liso = ", liso, "LnL=", log(value)))
        value
        }
}

Lnf3LeaveCache <- new.env(hash=TRUE)

Lnf3_leave <- function(alpha, delta, sigma, beta, tau, liso) {
        name <- paste("Leave", alpha, delta, sigma, beta, tau, liso)
        if (exists(name, env=Lnf3LeaveCache )){
#               cat("+")
#               flush.console()
                return(get(name,env=Lnf3LeaveCache ))
        } else {
#               cat(".")
                flush.console()

        z <- get_state_vectors_leave(c(),tau,liso)
        fn1 <- function(gamma) {

                fn0 <- function(states) {
                        Lnf1(gamma, sigma, beta, states, liso)
                }
```

```
                dev(gamma, alpha, delta)*sum(sapply(z,fn0))
        }

 lo <- qev(0.0005, alpha, delta)
        up <- qev(0.9995, alpha, delta)

        value <- nintegrate(fn1, lo, up)

        assign(name,value,Lnf3LeaveCache)
#       print(paste("Leave", "tau =", tau, "liso = ", liso, "LnL=", log(value)))
        value
        }
}

#
#       gq gets and caches the Gaussian quadrature points for numerical integration.
#       It relies on the gauss.quad() function of the statmod library.
#       statmod is available at http://cran.r-project.org.
#       Consult the documentation for your particular implementation of R
#       on how to install the statmod package.
#


gqCache <- new.env()

gq <- function(points) {
        name <- paste(points)
        if (exists(name, env=gqCache)){
                return(get(name,env=gqCache))
        } else {
                value <- gauss.quad(points)
                assign(name,value,gqCache)
                value
        }
}

IntegrationPoints <- 35

nintegrate <- function(fn1,a,b,points = IntegrationPoints){

        g <- gq(points)

        x <- ((b-a)/2)*g$nodes+((a+b)/2)
```

```
        w <- ((b-a)/2)*g$weights

        sum(sapply(x,fn1)*w)
}

#
#       my_plot2 plots the simulated cumulative retention curve for both ROTC
#       and the omitted group.
#

my_plot2<-function(alpha, delta, sigma, beta, w, v){
 myliso <- 9

 fn1 <- function(tau) {
        Lnf3_stay(-exp(alpha), exp(delta), exp(sigma), beta, tau, myliso)
 }

 t1 <- c(0:(30-myliso))
 y1 <- sapply(t1, fn1)

 fn2 <- function(tau) {
        Lnf3_stay(-exp(alpha+w), exp(delta+v), exp(sigma), beta, tau, myliso)
 }

 t2 <- c(0:(30-myliso))
 y2 <- sapply(t2, fn2)

 plot(myliso+t1,y1,type="s", col="red", ylim=c(0,1),
        ylab="Cumulative Retention Rate", xlab="YOS")

 lines(myliso+t2,y2,type="s", col="blue")

}




#
#       Lnf calculates the log likelihood for a particular observation, integrating out the
unobserved heterogeneity gamma
#

Lnf <- function(alpha, delta, sigma, beta, history, liso, final) {
```

```
        history <- history[!is.na(history)]
        tau <- length(history)
        if (tau > 0) { tau <- tau-1 }


        if (final=="Leave") {
                        v <- Lnf3 _ leave(alpha, delta, sigma, beta, tau, liso)
        } else {
                        v <- Lnf3 _ stay(alpha, delta, sigma, beta, tau, liso)
        }
        log(v)
}

best <- -100000
bestpars <- c(0,0,0)

ClearCache <- function(){
        VLCache <<- new.env(hash=TRUE)
        EVCache <<- new.env(hash=TRUE)
        Lnf3LeaveCache <<- new.env(hash=TRUE)
        Lnf3StayCache <<- new.env(hash=TRUE)
        PrStayCache <<- new.env(hash=TRUE)
}

DeleteCache <- TRUE

#
#       LnL calculates the log likelihood
#

LnL <- function(alpha, delta, sigma, beta, w, v){
#       try(save.image(file="workspace.RData"))

        if (DeleteCache) ClearCache()

        value <- 0
        cat(".")
        for (i in 1:length(freq)) {
                history <- c(as.character(y0[i]), as.character(y1[i]), as.character(y2[i]),
as.character(y3[i]), as.character(y4[i]), as.character(y5[i]), as.character(y6[i]))
                if (source[i]==2){source2<-1} else {source2<-0}
                y <- c(source2)
```

```
                value <- value + freq[i]*Lnf(-1*exp(alpha+sum(y*w)), exp(delta+sum(y*v)),
exp(sigma), beta, history, liso[i], as.character(final[i]))
                test <- (value==log(0))
                if (is.na(test)) return(log(0))
                if (test) return(log(0))
        }
        pars <- c(alpha, delta, sigma, w, v)
#       print(paste(" LnL(", paste(pars, collapse=","), ") = ", value))

        if (value > best) {
                best <<- value
                bestpars <<- pars
                my_plot2(alpha,delta,sigma,beta,w,v)
                cat("\n")
                print(paste("Best LnL(", paste(bestpars, collapse=","), ") = ", best))
        }


        value
}


#
#       fn is used to call the log likelihood function for the numerical
#       optimization routines
#

fn <- function(p) {
        -1*LnL(p[1], p[2], p[3], mybeta , c(p[4]),c(p[5]))
}

#
#       go does the maximum likelihood optimization, first using simulated
#       annealing, and then a hill-climbing algorithm. It stops when the
#       hill-climbing algorithm converges.
#

go <- function() {
        ClearCache()
        DeleteCache <<- TRUE
        try(out <- optim(bestpars, fn, hessian = FALSE, method="SANN",
                control=list(maxit=200,trace=100, REPORT=1)))
        out$convergence <-1
```

```
        for (i in 1:10){

                ClearCache()
                DeleteCache <<- FALSE
                try(out <- optim(bestpars, fn, hessian = FALSE, method="BFGS",
                        control=list(maxit=10, trace=100, REPORT=1)))

                if (exists("out")){
                        test <- (out$convergence==0)
                        if (is.na(test)) {
                        } else {
                                if(test) break
                        }
                }

                ClearCache()
                DeleteCache <<- TRUE
                try(out <- optim(bestpars, fn, hessian = FALSE, method="SANN",
                        control=list(maxit=200,trace=100, REPORT=1)))
                out$convergence <-1
        }
}

#
#       gradi calculates the value of the gradient for observation i
#


gradi <- function(alpha, delta, sigma, w2, v2, i){
        history <- c(as.character(y0[i]), as.character(y1[i]), as.character(y2[i]),
as.character(y3[i]), as.character(y4[i]), as.character(y5[i]), as.character(y6[i]))
        if (source[i]==2){source2<-1} else {source2<-0}
        if (source[i]==3){source3<-1} else {source3<-0}
        myenv <- new.env()

        assign("alpha",alpha,env=myenv)
        assign("delta",delta,env=myenv)
        assign("sigma",sigma,env=myenv)

        assign("w2",w2,env=myenv)
        assign("v2",v2,env=myenv)
```

```
        numericDeriv( quote(
                Lnf(-1*exp(alpha+w2*source2),exp(delta+v2*source2),
                exp(sigma),mybeta, history, liso[i], as.character(final[i]))),
                c("alpha", "delta", "sigma", "w2", "v2"), myenv)

}

#
#       bhhh calculates the standard errors using the sum of the outer product
#       of the gradients method.
#

bhhh <- function(alpha, delta, sigma, w2, v2){
        z <- matrix(0,nrow=5,ncol=5)
        for (i in 1:length(freq)) {
                x <- gradi(alpha, delta, sigma, w2, v2, i)
                y <- as.vector(attr(x,"gradient"))
                z <- z + freq[i]*outer(y,y)
                cat(".")
        }
        sqrt(abs(diag(solve(z))))
}
```

Listing 2—Example Program for Running DRM ACP

```
#
#       Sample program for running the DRM ACP
#       model.
#       It assumes that the basic model is stored in
#       the file "pilotmodel.R", and that the tab-delimited
#       data is stored in "newoccl.txt".

rm(list=ls())

try(detach("mydata"))
source("pilotmodel.R")

IntegrationPoints <- 35
#       Wc <- function(t) { pilotwages[t] }
Wc <- function(t) { percentile90th[t] }
temp <- read.table("newoccl.txt", header=TRUE)
mydata <- subset(temp,temp$liso>7)
attach(mydata)
print(mydata)
mybeta <- 0.90
#       mybeta <- 0.85
start <- c(4, 5, 6, -1, 0)
bestpars <- start

out <- go()
x <- bestpars
se <- bhhh(x[1],x[2],x[3],x[4],x[5])
```

Listing 3—Pilot Data

Tables B.1 and B.2 present the pilot data used by the authors. Table B.2 is a listing of the data used to estimate the dynamic retention model for pilots. It is stored in a tab-delimited file, with each record terminated with the end-of-line character appropriate to the computer operating system being used. The meaning of the codes is given in Table B.1.

Table B.1
Data Dictionary for Pilot Data

Variable	Definition
source	Source of accession: 1 = Academy, 2 = ROTC, 3 = Other
liso	Length of initial service obligation
final	Final disposition—did the officer stay or leave
sex	Gender, 0 = male, 1 = female
black	Race, 1 = black, 0 = white or other
freq	Frequency count of observations with these characteristics
y0–y6	State in a particular year, where the first two characters denote the rank of the officer, and the final two characters denote the year of service in which the officer was promoted to that rank. y0 corresponds to the year prior to the first decision point, y1 to the year of the first decision point, and so on.

Table B.2
Pilot Data

source	liso	final	sex	black	freq	y0	y1	y2	y3	y4	y5	y6
1	9	Leave	0	0	17	s304	s304	NA	NA	NA	NA	NA
1	9	Leave	0	0	139	s304	NA	NA	NA	NA	NA	NA
1	9	Leave	0	0	7	NA	NA	NA	NA	NA	NA	NA
1	9	Leave	0	0	4	NA	NA	NA	NA	NA	NA	NA
1	9	Leave	0	0	2	NA	NA	NA	NA	NA	NA	NA
1	9	Leave	0	0	1	s305	NA	NA	NA	NA	NA	NA
1	9	Stay	0	0	96	s304	s304	NA	NA	NA	NA	NA
1	9	Stay	0	0	249	s304	NA	NA	NA	NA	NA	NA
1	9	Stay	0	0	1	s305	s305	NA	NA	NA	NA	NA
2	9	Leave	0	0	29	s304	s304	NA	NA	NA	NA	NA
2	9	Leave	0	0	2	s304	NA	NA	NA	NA	NA	NA
2	9	Leave	0	0	3	s305	s305	NA	NA	NA	NA	NA
2	9	Leave	0	0	1	NA	NA	NA	NA	NA	NA	NA

Table B.2—Continued

source	liso	final	sex	black	freq	y0	y1	y2	y3	y4	y5	y6
2	9	Stay	0	0	32	s304	s304	NA	NA	NA	NA	NA
2	9	Stay	0	0	132	s304	NA	NA	NA	NA	NA	NA
2	9	Stay	0	0	3	s305	s305	NA	NA	NA	NA	NA
2	9	Stay	0	0	29	s305	NA	NA	NA	NA	NA	NA
1	9	Leave	0	1	2	s304	s304	NA	NA	NA	NA	NA
1	9	Leave	0	1	2	s304	NA	NA	NA	NA	NA	NA
1	9	Leave	0	1	1	NA	NA	NA	NA	NA	NA	NA
1	9	Stay	0	1	1	s304	s304	NA	NA	NA	NA	NA
1	9	Stay	0	1	8	s304	NA	NA	NA	NA	NA	NA
2	9	Stay	0	1	4	s304	NA	NA	NA	NA	NA	NA
2	9	Stay	0	1	1	s305	NA	NA	NA	NA	NA	NA
1	9	Leave	1	0	2	s304	s304	NA	NA	NA	NA	NA
1	9	Leave	1	0	7	s304	NA	NA	NA	NA	NA	NA
1	9	Stay	1	0	4	s304	s304	NA	NA	NA	NA	NA
1	9	Stay	1	0	16	s304	NA	NA	NA	NA	NA	NA
2	9	Leave	1	0	1	s304	s304	NA	NA	NA	NA	NA
2	9	Leave	1	0	1	NA	NA	NA	NA	NA	NA	NA
2	9	Stay	1	0	1	s304	s304	NA	NA	NA	NA	NA
2	9	Stay	1	0	4	s304	NA	NA	NA	NA	NA	NA
2	9	Stay	1	0	1	s305	s305	NA	NA	NA	NA	NA
1	8	Leave	0	0	1	s304	s304	s304	s304	s304	NA	NA
1	8	Leave	0	0	1	s304	NA	NA	NA	NA	NA	NA
1	8	Stay	0	0	2	s304	s304	s304	s304	s412	s412	NA
2	8	Leave	0	0	15	s304	s304	s304	s304	s304	NA	NA
2	8	Leave	0	0	1	s304	s304	s304	s304	s412	s412	NA
2	8	Leave	0	0	15	s304	s304	s304	s304	NA	NA	NA
2	8	Leave	0	0	14	s304	s304	s304	NA	NA	NA	NA
2	8	Leave	0	0	38	s304	s304	NA	NA	NA	NA	NA
2	8	Leave	0	0	67	s304	NA	NA	NA	NA	NA	NA
2	8	Stay	0	0	10	s304	s304	s304	s304	s412	s412	s412
2	8	Stay	0	0	120	s304	s304	s304	s304	s412	s412	NA

Table B.2—Continued

source	liso	final	sex	black	freq	y0	y1	y2	y3	y4	y5	y6
2	8	Stay	0	0	13	s304	s304	s304	s411	s411	s411	NA
2	8	Stay	0	0	1	s304	s304	s410	s410	s410	s410	NA
2	8	Stay	0	0	1	s304	s304	s411	s411	s411	s513	NA
2	8	Stay	0	0	2	s305	s305	s305	s305	s412	s412	NA
3	8	Leave	0	0	1	s304	s304	s304	s304	s304	s304	NA
3	8	Leave	0	0	5	s304	s304	s304	s304	s304	NA	NA
3	8	Leave	0	0	1	s304	s304	s304	s304	s412	s412	s412
3	8	Leave	0	0	2	s304	s304	s304	s304	NA	NA	NA
3	8	Leave	0	0	10	s304	s304	s304	NA	NA	NA	NA
3	8	Leave	0	0	1	s304	s304	s410	s410	s410	NA	NA
3	8	Leave	0	0	11	s304	s304	NA	NA	NA	NA	NA
3	8	Leave	0	0	37	s304	NA	NA	NA	NA	NA	NA
3	8	Stay	0	0	1	s304	s304	s304	s304	s304	s304	NA
3	8	Stay	0	0	3	s304	s304	s304	s304	s412	s412	s412
3	8	Stay	0	0	35	s304	s304	s304	s304	s412	s412	NA
3	8	Stay	0	0	2	s304	s304	s304	s411	s411	s411	NA
3	8	Stay	0	0	1	s304	s304	s410	s410	s410	s410	NA
1	8	Leave	0	1	1	s304	NA	NA	NA	NA	NA	NA
2	8	Leave	0	1	1	s304	s304	s304	NA	NA	NA	NA
2	8	Leave	0	1	1	s304	s304	NA	NA	NA	NA	NA
3	8	Leave	0	1	1	s304	NA	NA	NA	NA	NA	NA
3	8	Stay	0	1	1	s304	s304	s304	s304	s412	s412	NA
2	8	Stay	1	0	1	s304	s304	s304	s304	s412	s412	s412
2	8	Stay	1	0	1	s304	s304	s304	s304	s412	s412	NA
1	9	Leave	0	0	4	s304	s304	s304	s304	s304	NA	NA
1	9	Leave	0	0	3	s304	s304	s304	s304	s412	s412	NA
1	9	Leave	0	0	6	s304	s304	s304	s304	NA	NA	NA
1	9	Leave	0	0	2	s304	s304	s304	s412	s412	s412	NA
1	9	Leave	0	0	1	s304	s304	s304	s412	NA	NA	NA
1	9	Leave	0	0	12	s304	s304	s304	NA	NA	NA	NA
1	9	Leave	0	0	36	s304	s304	NA	NA	NA	NA	NA

Table B.2—Continued

source	liso	final	sex	black	freq	y0	y1	y2	y3	y4	y5	y6
1	9	Leave	0	0	83	s304	NA	NA	NA	NA	NA	NA
1	9	Stay	0	0	1	s304	s304	s304	s304	s304	NA	NA
1	9	Stay	0	0	2	s304	s304	s304	s304	s412	s412	s412
1	9	Stay	0	0	3	s304	s304	s304	s304	s412	s412	NA
1	9	Stay	0	0	1	s304	s304	s304	s412	s412	s412	s514
1	9	Stay	0	0	2	s304	s304	s304	s412	s412	s412	NA
1	9	Stay	0	0	62	s304	s304	s304	s412	s412	NA	NA
1	9	Stay	0	0	1	s304	s304	s411	s411	s411	s411	s514
1	9	Stay	0	0	1	s304	s304	s411	s411	s411	NA	NA
1	9	Stay	0	0	3	s304	s304	s412	s412	s412	NA	NA
2	9	Leave	0	0	19	s304	s304	s304	s304	NA	NA	NA
2	9	Leave	0	0	7	s304	s304	s304	NA	NA	NA	NA
2	9	Leave	0	0	10	s304	s304	NA	NA	NA	NA	NA
2	9	Leave	0	0	53	s304	NA	NA	NA	NA	NA	NA
2	9	Leave	0	0	1	s305	s305	s305	s305	s412	s412	NA
2	9	Leave	0	0	1	s305	s305	s305	s305	NA	NA	NA
2	9	Leave	0	0	3	s305	s305	s305	NA	NA	NA	NA
2	9	Leave	0	0	1	s305	s305	NA	NA	NA	NA	NA
2	9	Leave	0	0	3	s305	NA	NA	NA	NA	NA	NA
2	9	Stay	0	0	67	s304	s304	s304	s304	s412	s412	NA
2	9	Stay	0	0	1	s304	s304	s304	s412	s412	s412	s412
2	9	Stay	0	0	2	s304	s304	s304	s412	s412	s412	NA
2	9	Stay	0	0	18	s304	s304	s304	s412	s412	NA	NA
2	9	Stay	0	0	1	s304	s304	s410	s410	s410	s410	NA
2	9	Stay	0	0	1	s304	s304	s410	s410	s410	s513	NA
2	9	Stay	0	0	1	s304	s304	s411	s411	s411	NA	NA
2	9	Stay	0	0	5	s305	s305	s305	s305	s412	s412	NA
2	9	Stay	0	0	1	s305	s305	s305	s305	s413	s413	NA
2	9	Stay	0	0	1	s305	s305	s305	s412	s412	NA	NA
3	9	Leave	0	0	1	s304	s304	s304	NA	NA	NA	NA
3	9	Leave	0	0	1	s304	NA	NA	NA	NA	NA	NA

Table B.2—Continued

source	liso	final	sex	black	freq	y0	y1	y2	y3	y4	y5	y6
3	9	Stay	0	0	1	s304	s304	s304	s304	s304	NA	NA
3	9	Stay	0	0	1	s304	s304	s304	s412	s412	s412	s412
3	9	Stay	0	0	1	s304	s304	s304	s412	s412	s412	NA
3	9	Stay	0	0	4	s304	s304	s304	s412	s412	NA	NA
1	9	Leave	0	1	1	s304	s304	s304	s304	NA	NA	NA
1	9	Leave	0	1	2	s304	NA	NA	NA	NA	NA	NA
1	9	Stay	0	1	2	s304	s304	s304	s412	s412	NA	NA
3	9	Stay	0	1	1	s304	s304	s304	s412	s412	NA	NA
1	9	Leave	1	0	1	s304	s304	NA	NA	NA	NA	NA
1	9	Leave	1	0	6	s304	NA	NA	NA	NA	NA	NA
2	10	Leave	0	0	1	s304	s304	NA	NA	NA	NA	NA
2	10	Stay	0	0	2	s304	s304	s304	s412	s412	NA	NA
2	10	Stay	0	0	1	s304	s304	s412	s412	s412	s412	NA
3	10	Leave	1	0	1	s304	NA	NA	NA	NA	NA	NA

Bibliography

Ausink, John A. and David A. Wise, "The Military Pension, Compensation, and Retirement of U.S. Air Force Pilots," working paper, Cambridge, Mass.: National Bureau of Economic Research, W4593, December 1993.

Daula, Thomas, and Robert Moffitt, "Estimating Dynamic Retention Model of Quit Behavior: The Case of Military Reenlistment," *Journal of Labor Economics*, Vol. 13, No. 3, July 1995, pp. 499–523.

Dempster, Arthur, Nan Laird, and Donald Rubin. "Maximum Likelihood from Incomplete Data via the EM Algorithm," *Journal of the Royal Statistical Society, Series B (Methodological)*, Vol. 39, No. 1, 1977, pp. 1–38.

Department of the Air Force, *Aviator Continuation Pay (ACP) Program*, Air Force Instruction 36-3004, Washington, D.C., February 24, 2000.

Fernandez, Richard L., Glenn A. Gotz, and Robert M. Bell, *The Dynamic Retention Model*, Santa Monica, Calif.: RAND Corporation, N-2141-MIL, 1985. As of March 21, 2007: http://www.rand.org/pubs/notes/N2141/

Goldberg, Matthew S., "A Survey of Enlisted Retention: Models and Findings," Chapter II in U.S. Department of Defense, Office of the Under Secretary of Defense for Personnel and Readiness, *Report of the Ninth Quadrennial Review of Military Compensation*, Vol III: *Creating Differentials in Military Pay: Special and Incentive Pays*, Washington, D.C., 2002, pp. 65–134.

Gotz, Glenn A., and John Joseph McCall, *A Dynamic Retention Model for Air Force Officers: Theory and Estimates*, Santa Monica, Calif.: RAND Corporation, R-3028-AF, 1984. As of March 21, 2007: http://www.rand.org/pubs/reports/R3028/

Hogan, Paul, and Matthew Black, "Reenlistment Models: A Methodological Review," in Curtis Gilroy, David Horne, and D. Alton Smith, eds., *Military Compensation and Personnel Retention: Models and Evidence*, U.S. Army Research Institute for the Behavioral and Social Sciences, 1991, pp. 19–42.

Hogan, Paul F., and Javier Espinoza, *A Model of Air Force Officer Retention*, technical report, Alexandria, Va.: Human Resources Research Organization, TR-02-65, 2003.

Hosek, James R., Michael Mattock, C. Christine Fair, Jennifer Kavanagh, Jennifer Sharp, and Mark E. Totten, *Attracting the Best: How the Military Competes for Information Technology Personnel*, Santa Monica, Calif.: RAND Corporation, MG-108-OSD, 2004. As of March 21, 2007: http://www.rand.org/pubs/monographs/MG108/

Neal, Radford, and Geoffrey Hinton, "A View of the EM Algorithm That Justifies Incremental, Sparse, and Other Variants," in Michael I. Jordan, ed., *Learning in Graphical Models*, Cambridge, Mass.: MIT Press, 1999, pp. 355–368.

R Development Core Team, *R: A Language and Environment for Statistical Computing*, computer language, Vienna, Austria: R Foundation for Statistical Computing, 2005. As of March 21, 2007: http://www.r-project.org/